Universal Grace: Myth or Reality?

Richard G. Cote

ORBIS BOOKS

Maryknoll, New York 10545

234.1
C843u

Library of Congress Cataloging in Publication Data

Cote, Richard G   1934–
    Universal grace.

    1. Grace (Theology) I. Title.
BT761.2.C66   234'.1   77-5570
ISBN 0-88344-521-2

Orbis Books, Maryknoll, New York 10545

78-4939

Printed in the United States of America

Universal Grace: Myth or Reality?

*The Incarnation is the renewal,
the restoration, of all the energies
and powers of the universe.*

—Teilhard de Chardin

Contents

Introduction

Words can gain religious significance with time; but they can also lose it. In the living tradition of language, no word is ever confirmed in its meaning once and for all. The word "grace" is no exception.

To modern secularized people divine grace is a stupendous fantasy that cannot speak to our contemporary situation. It neither touches them nor enters into the normal course of their concerns and experience. Even Christians today are finding it increasingly difficult to square the spiritual reality of grace with their everyday experience. Many Christians feel deep in their hearts how hollow and devoid of religious content this word has become for them. They may cling nostalgically to this concept that occupied a central place in the religious instruction of their childhood, but in their moments of clarity they are obliged to admit that the truth and reality of grace now seem as distant as an echo, no longer vibrating in their souls as in the past. Like a tide receding from the seashore, grace withdraws from us and deposits us on the sands of a secularized world.

Within the vast area of theological renewal thrown up by the Second Vatican Council, the need for a new theology of grace has become increasingly clear. Commenting on the dogmatic constitution *Lumen Gentium*, Karl Rahner has aptly indicated the task that faces theologians: "Theology will have to show how divine grace is not simply the intermittent chance of salvation of an individual kind granted to a few only and restricted in time and place, but that it is ultimately the dynamism of all human history everywhere and always, and indeed of the world generally" (*The Christian of the Future*, p. 96).

The aim of our investigations is to show how the world is penetrated and filled with God's grace; how the daily life and ordinary existence of all people is in fact impregnated with it; how this grace gives us solidarity with all people, binds us mysteriously together, and makes us share in the common fate of all. In short, our inquiry concerns *universal grace* precisely as emerging, through the continuing effects of the Incarnation, from the inmost center of humanity and the world and giving meaning to all that we experience, enact, and suffer in the process of living and dying. More specifically, our efforts will be to describe the historical background of the new thinking on universal grace, to provide a personalist basis for its justification, and to say what consequences follow for a church that takes universal grace seriously.

Hence the first part of our book will examine the basis for the concept of universal grace, while the second part will deal with its practical implications with respect to four burning issues in the church today. These are the problems: Is there any essential difference between the grace of Christians and that of non-Christians or nonbelievers? (2) If universal grace is present and at work in the world at large, how are we to envisage the relationship between the church and the world? (3) If the concept of universal grace is accepted, how is the present dichotomy between "evangelization" and "development" to be overcome? (4) If universal grace *is* taken seriously, what are the future prospects of the church in developing countries? For the consideration of this last question I have selected the particular area of Africa. In the course of our discussion of these problems it is important that the reader have constantly in mind the particular view of universal grace taken in the first chapters, for that necessarily determines the kind of answers we shall be able to give to these questions.

The root conviction of this book is that universal grace is a reality operative in a secular world as well as in a sacred temple. Even before the church's missionary intervention, the effects of the Incarnation have been applied to all people. All people, baptized or not, militant atheist or atheist in daily practice, are born not only in original sin but in original grace as well, a state which constitutes for us an abiding, transforming influence of Christ. "For if by the offense of the one man all died, much more did the grace of God and the gracious gift of the one man, Jesus Christ, abound for all" (Rom. 5:15). In other words, we shall try to come to grips with the question of the wider reaches of God's saving activity outside the visible boundaries of the church.

Our approach to grace will not only be bold; it will be boldly personalist—grace seen and experienced as the quality of interpersonal relationships. Certainly one of the main currents of thought forming the language and mode of expression of our day is personalism. At all times, but especially today, our innermost (if not outmost!) being revolts against all forms of human exploitation, managed humanity, impersonal society; against all tendencies that would rob human beings of their true meaning. Before all else, the success or failure of our lives depends on the quality of our personal relationships with others, whether other people or God. Hence we shall consider grace not as it is situated in the human soul as such but as it is situated in the inner space between persons. Here it admits various degrees of immediacy and intimacy; it sinks to all levels of the personal order and is rooted in them.

Universal grace rises like the sap of a tree in the one trunk of humanity and spreads throughout the branches of the personal order. Indeed this all-pervasive quality is what makes grace so "ordinary": It loses itself in the commonplaceness of daily life. It is simply the ultimate depth of everything that we do when we try to achieve authentic existence—when we accept responsibility, stand up for truth, hope against hope, cheerfully refuse to be embittered by the stupidity of life, break out of our ego-center to help our neighbor; when, in a word, we have the quiet courage to support the existence of others, endure long with them, live with them and grant them, ever anew and differently, our total presence. This is where grace occurs, because all this leads us into the mystery of Christ.

Something else must be said about this grace that circulates so unobtrusively in the veins of our everyday life. It has its source in Jesus Christ who, like us, led a life full of ordinariness—birth, hardship, courage, hope, failure, and death. A theology of grace, therefore, can find its real basis only in the Incarnation. By becoming a person among people, the Son of God does not merely dip his finger into history; he immerses himself totally in the human community of persons. Hence everything we shall say about universal grace will be the direct result of having gazed on Christ's insertion into the three strata of our personal order: how he (1) assumes the radical bond-in-being that unites all people, (2) shares our human solidarity, and (3) actively enters into the wide world of human encounters and relationships. Nothing of any real significance can ever be said of grace that does not stem from Christ's personal experience as a being-in-the-world. Since the Son of God descended vertically into the deeper world of human subjectivity, the first and last word about divine grace is Christ's "I am with you." We must descend to such depths of the personal order to understand how thoroughly grounded divine grace is in the modern secular world and how universally it is at work in it.

Without doubt our attempt to allow the mystery of God's love to display itself anew in the epiphany of modern thought patterns is a risk-laden task. This is so not only because of the possibility of human error; more fundamentally it is so because of the divine risk that the Word of God has taken in assuming a thoroughly human nature. No amount of theologizing will ever make the undertaking safer. Yet to shy away from our task because of the danger is like staying home because accidents occur on the street. Theologians must go out on the limb because that is where the fruit grows. It is on such ventures that the vitality of theology depends; otherwise it becomes merely a sort of domestic housekeeping. Theologians spend their time talking *about* their theology, explaining themselves to themselves. This can be particularly self-defeating when the topic under discussion is divine grace.

I think that some such approach and some such conclusions as we shall reach in this book are desperately needed today in the interests of ecumenism. Certainly one of the deepest points of division between Christians has long been the question of grace. Yet the point of departure for an ecumenically minded theology of grace cannot be the attempt to reconcile the Catholic and Protestant formulations of the past. They belong to the thought patterns of earlier ages. Since, moreover, they arose for the most part in the context of controversy they are definitions of disputed points of doctrine rather than expressions of teaching on grace in its fullness.

Nor if, after so many years of reproachful division, the various Christian communities were to "pool" the truthful statements about grace that they have in common and discard all their prejudices would the result be "the whole truth and nothing but the truth." In this important respect, as Norman Pittinger has suggested, Christian truth takes exception to the law of mathematics that the total is equal to the sum of the parts. And this is, first of all, because it is basically the truth of a Promise—therefore a reality still in process; and secondly because the demand of this truth is not something "to have and to hold," like a possession in life, but something to seek and strive after, a vocation, an adventure, an openness toward the future. To have lost this *sense of adventure* in our theology of grace is to have lost an essential part of it. The theology of grace we are proposing requires a new vision, one that can only be seen with new and ever more perfect eyes. In view of Christ's self-communication and abiding presence in the world, it will become abundantly clear how God, with the whole of creation dependent upon him, can still love every person personally as though he had nothing else to do.

PART ONE

A THEOLOGY OF UNIVERSAL GRACE

1

Historical Perspective

The historical background of this new thinking on universal grace is important. Without this historical perspective, one might get the false impression that the contemporary focus upon the problem of universal grace is something that came as a sudden inspiration to modern theologians. What is in fact involved is a slow and lengthy process of rediscovery, often determined more by the times than by the theologians themselves. For in viewing grace once more in its social dimension, theological thought is reverting to the communitarian concept of grace that characterized the primitive church. The early church saw the individual's fall from grace as weakening the bonds within the whole community: the sense that God saves individuals not as individuals but as members of his people was still very much alive. To trace the historical course of development whereby this communitarian concept of grace has become the individualistic one prevailing until our own time would be outside the scope of this book. If it is kept in mind that central Christian teaching is inevitably modified by cultural change, a brief résumé of some of the developments of modern times will suffice.

Individualistic Grace

It seems fair to say that the trend toward an individualistic concept of grace that had its roots in the early Middle Ages but was strengthened in the centuries following the Reformation peaked in the nineteenth century. A variety of factors had converged in western society to produce people who regarded themselves as independent and self-reliant individuals. Their strutting self-assurance was buoyed up by the heritage of literature and philosophy that had become easily available to them as well as by the industrial society in which they worked. Philosophers like Jean-Jacques Rousseau and Thomas Hobbes had long since convinced people that society was little more than an aggregate of individuals who had come together as a necessary means of survival. Defoe's *Robinson Crusoe*—that fictional depiction of splendid human autonomy—happily assured them that if ever bad came to worse in society they could survive on their own. Curiously, it was not on a desert island but in a crowded industrial society that they would exercise their sense of freedom and autonomy.

This exaggerated individualism that failed to acknowledge the social nature of human beings inevitably took its toll on religious thought and ethics. Religion was conceived as the narrow path to personal salvation. It was always an intensely personal affair between God and the individual (to the exclusion of the Christian community), the privileged point of encounter being the center of the individual soul.

There is, of course, much to recommend such an inward-looking spirituality. Like the art of sculpture, Christian life is in many respects an interiorizing process. Sculptors must discover and liberate the statue deeply embedded within the piece of wood or marble. They do this painstakingly, working their way into the crude material. Similarly Christians discover and encounter God deep within their hearts. In order to live continually in the presence of God, Christians strive to live a more interior life. This will always remain true. However, what is to be deplored in the religious outlook of the last century is the exclusive preoccupation with the moral questions of personal sin, personal virtue, and individual uprightness. Little or no thought was given to the life of the Christian community and the way God saves individuals, not as individuals, but as participants in God's kingdom, in the unity of a "people."

This exaggerated tendency in Christian thought to exalt individuals and their rights had serious repercussions in both Protestantism and Catholicism. In Protestantism it had the effect of renewing the fragmentation that had begun at the time of the Reformation, resulting in a multitude of splinter groups or sects, each committed to some special emphasis of interpretation of Scripture on the basis of private judgment. Corporate loyalty was little more than the tenuous association of sympathetic or like-minded Christians. It was merely the voluntary fellowship of those who existed initially as Christian individuals.

Another consequence of this individualist understanding within Protestantism, having its beginnings in the seventeenth century but very much alive in the nineteenth, was pietism. The sect easily becomes another Noah's ark, sealed within and without so that it can come safely through the flood. Such restrictions contradict the very nature of grace. The danger lies in a self-righteous separation from the world instead of being the light of the world and the salt of the earth. If God has blessed his people with a signal outpouring of grace, this must be so that Christians shall be better able to recognize and strengthen all manifestations of grace in the world.

Individualistic grace was no less present in the Catholic church. Within a theology and preaching strongly influenced by the prevailing atmosphere of individualism, grace was all too often presented almost in quantitative terms, rather like a substance in the soul that could be increased by good behavior. The loss of sanctifying grace was regarded like the loss of any item of one's personal effects, with the effect upon the Christian community not adverted to unless the sinner was a public sinner.

At worst, this understanding of grace produced a striving for personal perfection in which the "spiritual life" became something quite alien to the laws of human psychology. In the view of the anxious penitent, grace could be fully alive on Tuesday, dead on Friday, fully alive again on Saturday afternoon, only to die again on Monday morning. This "off and on" idea of grace meant that it could die and climb out of its grave with the frequency with which one climbs out of the bathtub. It also meant that grace was an enrichment of the individual soul and the means of personal salvation—an outlook reflected in the expression "saving one's soul." All in all, it was an extremely private achievement that left little room for the social, more universal character of grace.

In much nineteenth-century theologizing the traditional theological distinction between *objective* and *subjective* redemption was interpreted in a way inimical to the church's universal mission. The basic idea in this distinction is that with the completion of Christ's redeeming acts on earth all people were virtually—that is, in principle—saved: Grace was now available to us, within reach, "at hand." This objective redemption is subjectively applied when the individual freely accepts the grace of Christ as God's self-communication. Although from the early Middle Ages the church had taught that those not reached by the preaching of the gospel could receive saving grace through the "baptism of desire," this was largely lost sight of in the prevailing view of grace as an individual matter. Objective redemption was vaguely conceived as some infinite "deposit" of saving grace—which was presumably stored in heaven—and before anyone could draw from this store of living water the distribution of baptism was necessary. This restricted view of baptism as a narrow aqueduct of saving grace quite naturally led Christians to think very pessimistically of the salvation of non-Christians. Such a narrowly conceived dispensation of divine grace all but precluded the truth of universal grace.

Leaning heavily on an analogy that had not only found favor with St. Thomas but had long since been canonized at the Council of Quiercy, theologians of the last century made much of Christ's redeeming acts as a remedy against sin. And like all remedies prepared well in advance, Christ's redemption could produce its remedial effects only when actually applied to the wounds of each sinful individual. Such picture-taking, with all its advantages in expressing imponderables, has its own corresponding limitations and can never be theologically exact unless viewed in the light of other scriptural and patristic images. The early fathers of the church had indeed pictured Christ as a Doctor, a Good Samaritan, pouring oil and wine on the gaping wounds of humankind. According to them, however, Christ was not merely preparing a remedy for humankind during his earthly life; he was actually in the process of healing and saving all people. As one of them put it, "It is distinctive of a true and charitable physician to live among the sick, *and not leave them before they are cured.*" Little theological reflection was given to this rich stream of patristic imagery, and still less effort was made to develop a theology of enduring grace present universally and at work everywhere in all members of humankind.

This restrictive view of grace produced yet another distortion in the Christian thinking of the last century. I refer to the stress, in infant baptism, placed on the necessity of releasing the infant from the insidious power of Satan. In the logic of this kind of theological thinking, one would surmise that Adam had a more direct and devastating influence over people than had Christ. As we shall see, nothing could be more contrary to the unbroken teaching and tradition of the church.

Theologians were consequently faced once again with the thorny and recurrent problem of infants dying without baptism. Their discussions did have the merit of safeguarding—however indirectly or obliquely—the doctrine concerning the universality of grace. The teaching that it is God's will that all people should be saved, along with the fact that Christ died for all, does call for a means of salvation that is physically and morally possible for all, including unbaptized infants. This crucial point, however, was polemically obscured and soon lost in elaborate theological abstractions. Later one would hear an occasional voice crying in the wilderness, such as that of Abbé Boudes (the reader is not expected to have ever heard of him!), who maintained that the bond of solidarity between Christ and the human race far exceeds anything like that which may exist between Adam and his posterity. Unfortunately the focus on this solidarity was quickly blurred and the whole question of universal grace remained hopelessly on the periphery of the ensuing theological discussions.

Our religious sense as Christians today is different. We find it difficult to suppose that people who have never heard of Christ do not stand in a positive relationship with him. In many respects, the Second Vatican Council marks a decisive milestone. Not only does it tell us that God is mercifully at work among the peoples beyond the boundaries of the church and that even the atheist is somehow under the loving influence of divine grace, but it affirms a pre-given engracement of all people: "For by his Incarnation, the Son of God has united himself in some fashion with every man." Taking this theological axiom over from tradition, the Council made no attempt to explain its meaning. A discreet omission, it challenges theologians to scale the truth of this bold affirmation just as a silent, beckoning mountain would challenge any stalwart mountain climber.

In this new context, we must try to understand how all people are united and present to Christ and stand in a positive relationship to grace. This revives an old dilemma. On the one hand, most theologians today are convinced that the Incarnation profoundly affects human and cosmic life in all its aspects; for them it is inconceivable that any area of human endeavor should be unaffected by grace. On the other hand, if the world truly belongs to Christ and people are already, at birth, in a graced union with Christ, how are we to understand the role and mission of the church in the world?

A more personalist approach to grace will enable us to resolve this dilemma. We shall see that the hitherto conceived "primary" order of the Incarnate Word and the "subsequent" order of grace are in fact but one and the same saving reality. It is curious and doubtless providential that two movements of modern thought, at first glance contradictory, are today coming into vital confrontation in our effort to adopt a less individualistic concept of grace and a new Christian posture before the world and its values: the new emphasis on human solidarity and the philosophy of the person. We will briefly consider both of these.

Human Solidarity

Humankind today evinces a growing tendency to unification and is becoming increasingly aware of its solidarity. Let us take a closer look at some of the symptoms of this phenomenon. Consider in the first place the influence of modern communications and the rapprochement brought about by industry, trade, and commerce on a world scale. Technology, which has increased world production, distribution, and consumption, has virtually wiped out the frontiers that formerly separated individuals, countries, and peoples. In every sphere of human endeavor we see humankind striving to realize its intrinsic oneness. Deep within the human conscience today is the conviction that the individual does not stand alone. More and more we are beginning to see the problems and needs of the minority as the task and challenge of the majority. Even the hunger, poverty, and illiteracy of the world's majority are weighing increasingly on the conscience of the world's privileged few. Tyranny, poverty, disease, overpopulation, and war itself can no longer be contained within the neat confines of geographical boundaries. Pandora's box has been opened, and isolationism seems irretrievably a thing of the past.

Every nation, without exception now, finds itself implicated and involved in whatever is happening in the world. Every war, however limited, becomes a world war, not only because the peace of the world is threatened but because world peace is broken. It is no longer possible to speak realistically of "hot spots" in this or that country since the world is at one with itself. The dreadful threat of total war and total destruction makes everyone keenly aware that their lives and destinies are bound closely together.

Every scientific or medical breakthrough — whether it occurs on the launching pads at Cape

Kennedy or in the sterilized wards at Groote Schuur Hospital in South Africa—has immediate, world-wide repercussions. Never before in the history of humankind has it been possible for the attention of virtually every human being on earth to be riveted on the same event at the same time. When a prominent head of state like President Kennedy is assassinated, the world stands still in a state of shock; when a relatively unknown man like Neil Armstrong sets foot on the moon's surface for the first time, the world is wrapped in awe as people around the globe get a detailed coverage of the event on television sets or transistor radios.

People have never before been so conscious of living, working, and dying together on the same planet. They have never been so painfully reminded that 80 percent of the world's resources are at the disposal of only 20 percent of the people; that the rich are growing richer and the poor are left with little hope of breaking out of their stagnation in the next decades. The riots, marches, demonstrations, and other forms of conscientious objection, which have become a telling sign of our times in the face of glaring inequalities and injustices, sharpen our sense of unity in a cruel way. The most serious danger to humanity today is that it should allow its awakening sense of unity to be absorbed and lost in the bitter disputes and conflicts that are rending the world, dividing it into opposing camps.

We are plainly bent on creating organizational structures and international bodies to promote world peace, justice, and development. The United Nations is but a feeble and often capricious expression of this deep aspiration. Admittedly there is still much to be done in the way of making what are often the token symbols of our ulitmate dream become a reality. The important thing is that we have a dream. Beneath the surface of these world programs and deep within the tensions and conflicts that surround them, there lies the unseen, more intrinsic reality of humankind's oneness.

No modern church leader has insisted more on the unity of the human race than Pius XII, whose words are perhaps better understood today than when he spoke them. In his first encyclical letter, his keynote address as it were, the pope outlined the Christian basis for understanding the solidarity of humankind. He saw it as a given reality and a task to be carried out. We are never so completely alone, so individual and set apart by ourselves even in the most extraordinary circumstances, that our decisions and deeds have no repercussion in the world around us. Human solidarity is above all a spiritual reality: Together with all other people, we stand before God as a family, a community of persons.

The term "solidarity" has also reverberated down the corridors of modern political economy and sociology. As the leitmotiv of the social doctrine called "solidarism," it signified the obligation of mutual assistance, of standing side by side in the face of a social task. As a reaction against individualism, this doctrine emphasized the social nature of human beings, but in its effort to avoid the trap of collectivism it did not go far enough. It failed to see that our being is fully encompassed by being-social and that solidarity is not so much a special function of our life as the dimension of depth in all our functions.

In the meantime, theologians were busy introducing the concept of solidarity in their interpretation of the propagation of original sin and using it to clarify the idea of expiation and atonement. In Protestant theology, this borrowed concept developed more along ethico-moral lines whereas in Catholic theology it was to remain more a linguistic graft than a working theological principle. The trend in modern thought toward personalism was already under way, and this new philosophy was to have a more radical influence in reshaping theology generally and in rehabilitating the doctrine of universal grace in particular.

The Personal Order

Existential philosophy and recent psychological research have shown that the human person neither stands alone nor is complete in itself. It now appears very clearly that a person—*as* person—must be understood and defined in relation to other persons. The recovery of perspective that such findings have made possible in the theology of grace cannot be easily exaggerated. The point is that not only is the structure of the classical treatise on grace affected, but it is reanchored as to its very basis. Increased scope is thus given to the personal character of grace: More than just a gift to the individual person, grace is seen as a relationship between persons. Before considering more recent developments in the theology of grace, we should first recall how we have developed in consciousness of ourselves as persons.

Historically, the scientific discovery of nature was followed by people's discovery of themselves; or, to put it differently, the discovery of outer space eventually led to the discovery of inner space. The simplicity of this statement conceals at least two far-reaching revolutions in our understanding. The first was the scientific revolution of the seventeenth century. The really significant feature of this revolution is that we began to look at the world of nature with new eyes. Not only were new facts about the world brought to light and old facts seen in a new perspective, but through the coupling of mathematics with observation, induction, and controlled experiment, a new worldview emerged. There is no doubt that this new vision of cosmic reality contributed to people's discovery of themselves. As they discovered the laws of nature, people gained self-assurance and felt less abandoned to unknown cosmic forces. Relying more and more on their ability to measure and predict these forces, they suddenly realized that they could to some extent control nature. In the past, they had to conform to nature; now they reckoned that they could make nature conform to their needs and desires, and with this new possibility came a sense of liberation and self-possession.

The second important revolution to which we refer did not occur until the nineteenth century when scientific method was applied to human history. The careful, disciplined, and objective study of history enabled people to discover their real place in nature. We can say that people finally found themselves by discovering their own footprints in the sands of time. No longer a mere biological fragment of nature, human beings emerged as ones who transform both the world around them and their own nature through culture. Thus they "came alive" against the impersonal background of the cosmos they had long been observing.

This new awareness of making history was a big step in human self-understanding. It was like coming of age. Existence became more transparent and a new harmony was evolved. Yet mature people, whose thoughts and feelings are more sober, gradually become more critical regarding their relationships with other persons. The fissures and contradictions that divide people begin to appear in a new light. Similarly the dawn of personalism came to light against the brutalizing background of industrialism. The industrial society often reduced men, women, and children to mere automatons. It tended to deal with masses instead of persons, to value individuals for what they could do rather than for themselves, and to substitute a system or process of production for personal relations. Revolting against these social losses, personalism championed the value of persons and developed into a philosophy over the last four decades, especially in Germany and France. Prior to this new thinking, a personalist theology of grace could not have been constructed; in the present world of thought its emergence is inevitable.

New Theology of Grace

Recent trends involving the use of personalist categories to describe the reality of grace have evolved largely during the past ten years. Our intention here is not to review the considerable amount of writing in this field, but to indicate the general direction in which theologians are moving. Their main avenue of progress lies in a converging effort to explain grace in terms of human experience. This means, first of all, that theologians themselves must have a certain experience of grace if, at all, they are to speak about grace in an authentic and honest way. The theologians' lives are in fact far from being defined in terms of research, reading, and reflection alone. Their field of experimentation and verification is human experience, because divine grace meets the world of today in the midst of the preoccupations of daily life. The awareness of their own, and others', experience of alienation, of doubt, of faith, and of the presence

and absence of God is terribly important in understanding grace. The truth of grace grows primarily
by being lived and experienced: obeyed, disobeyed;
doubted, found good; rejoiced in, suffered in.
Hence the conviction among modern theologians
that grace must be studied in the *clair-obscur* of
human experience.

Second, in their efforts to reach the truth of grace
as a living experience, theologians are turning more
than ever to specialists on matters of human
psychology. This holds true of Protestant as well as
Catholic theologians. The exciting thing is that in
this particular area theologians are dissipating the
myth of the distant professor, lost to the divinity he
or she claims to study. Among Protestant theologians, one would have to mention Paul Tillich, who
was greatly influenced by psychology. His many
relevant writings include *The Theological Significance
of Existentialism and Psychoanalysis.* Following Tillich, Thomas Oden proposes a psychologically
oriented theology in *Kerygma and Counseling* and in
Contemporary Theology and Psychotherapy. A similar
approach is found in the works of Don S. Brown-
ing, particularly his *Atonement and Psychotherapy,*
where the therapeutic process is offered as a model
for the understanding of soteriology.

Catholic theologians too have found modern
psychology a useful source for the development of a
new theology of grace. William W. Meissner, for
example, in his book *Foundations for a Psychology of
Grace,* draws quite heavily from many well-known

psychologists. He brings into focus the central idea that grace acts in people as an energizing dynamism that makes them progressively more fully free and fully human. Similarly, Peter Fransen, in his comprehensive work *The New Life of Grace,* extends the psychology of grace to the limits of the Christian experience. Gregory Baum is yet another theologian whose insights into grace have been remarkably influenced by modern psychology. In a recent book, *Man Becoming: God in Secular Language,* especially in the section titled "Redemptive Immanence," the author comes as close as any in constructing a theology of grace in purely personalist terms. The really significant development is the fact that Catholic and Protestant theologians are reflecting on grace along converging lines. One does not have to be a great prophet to see the truly exciting possibilities such a convergence announces for ecumenism. We should mention, however, two important drawbacks in the present development.

The first criticism often made is that some writers use a personalist approach—but only sometimes and somewhat, not fully and consistently. I could not agree more fully. Many do make considerable use of psychological categories, but fail really to use them as the framework or keystone of their theological construction. The result is that the classical concepts of grace are merely translated (not interpreted) into new words and modes of speech. It is as though old wine is being poured into new wineskins, and this is never entirely satisfactory.

We cannot simply accept past theological statements about grace, tied up as they are in their objective meaning with an outdated world-picture and philosophy, and merely translate them into new categories. Much more is required, which brings us to a second objection.

A more serious question is whether or not this new approach to grace can ever be anything more than an "approach"—a description rather than a definition of grace, a perspective rather than a theology of grace. Since grace is the way God acts in and through persons, attempts to understand grace according to the viewpoint and method of human psychology are indeed legitimate. They do bring home to us in yet another way the genuineness and the extent of God's incarnate love, which enables us to grow in openness and humanness. Nevertheless, it is my firm conviction that human psychology alone can never serve as an adequate basis and framework for a theology of grace. Something more is required—indeed something else is possible, namely, a view of grace below the surface and depths of human psychology. This will take us, in the next chapter, beneath the psychology of human relationships as such and deep into the ontological subsoil of personhood. The detailed examination of the personal order at this deeper level may at first seem forbidding, but it will only postpone a little the joy of contemplating the spiritual riches of grace and will support the hope of a better and more meaningful theology of universal grace.

2

"I Am With You"

It has always been the firm conviction of Christian faith that the Incarnation—Christ's "I am with you"—is the renewal, the restoration, of all the energies and powers of the universe. Through his incarnation, the Son of God united himself in a most radical way with people—indeed with every person. Universal grace, and the radical salvation it bestows, can best be described as Christ's abiding presence in the human personal order, that is, in the community of persons that constitutes humankind. Before we explore the implications of Christ's involvement in the personal web of humankind, it is important first to see the Incarnation in its proper perspective. This will enable us to understand better both the significance of the Christian assertion that all people stand in a grace-full relationship with Christ, and also the significance of the further assertion that this abiding state of universal grace refers directly and for all people to the risen Lord.

"Redemptive" Incarnation

Studies of modern scholars reveal that to the mind of the early fathers of the church the Incarnation was not merely a launching pad, a point of departure in the scheme of salvation, as it were a prelude to redemption. Rather, the Incarnation was conceived as a continuous, dynamic "taking-on" by the Son of God of all the ordinary events and conditions that make up human existence—birth and toil, bravery and hope, failure and death. Thus the entire life of Christ and his everyday acts established the Incarnation in its unfolding aspect, its authenticity, and its full efficacy.

Having lost sight of this all-embracing dynamism with respect to the doctrine of the Incarnation, theologians not unsurprisingly came to develop the doctrine of the Redemption quite independently of it. The sacrifice of Christ on the cross was viewed as the principle and source of salvation, while the Incarnation was generally seen as a necessary precondition "in view" of the cross. Hence one of the burning questions was whether or not the Incarnation was redemptive in the strict sense of the word. The emphasis was placed by and large on the redemptive *motive* of the Incarnation rather than on its redemptive value as such. The ensuing debates saw theologians sadly pitting the Latin fathers against the Greek fathers. The fact is, however, that notwithstanding their originality and differences in character, mentality, and tradition, the fathers all basically concur on the redemptive nature of the Incarnation.

Another important point in their teaching was that Christ's all-assuming incarnation heals and restores human nature. No area of human existence, whether physiological or psychological, was left untouched and unaffected by the grace of the incarnate Word. The Incarnation and the instant restoring grace that it released and injected into the veins of human life radically restores the human condition for all people of all times. The Son of God chose to become a human being in order to save humankind as a human being, from within, "renewing man in man." The Savior was not merely to be a gift from on high, but he was, as the "fruit of the earth" (Isa. 4:2), to bud forth from the earth like a plant (Isa. 45:8). Thus the Incarnation was tantamount to a transfusion of new life, new energy, and new hope into the bloodstream of the already existing arteries of humankind. Underlying this view of the Incarnation as a divine transfusion from within is a forceful affirmation of the unity of humankind.

It was in the light of Christ's entry into this basic unity that the early fathers explained the radical solidarity between Christ and all people, a union they described as affording all a real and enduring measure of grace. In this view, there is not a single person who could be isolated from the community of the human race. The incarnation of God in the man Christ was therefore seen as a union of God with the whole body of humankind. Admittedly the fathers never stopped to consider this saving bond-in-being for itself, but always viewed it in relation to that more perfect union established through faith, baptism, and the Eucharist. For them our radical solidarity with Christ is a state of grace whose ultimate meaning is fully disclosed only in the personal acknowledgement of the Word made flesh. They saw it as a divine force in the world leading to a mode of activity proper to it. But they never set up a frontier (as later theologians would do) between the community of nature—however graced—on the one hand, and the ecclesial community of the faith on the other. They always envisaged the whole community of humankind—not just the Christian community—as caught up in the consequences of the Incarnation, involved in and affected by everything Christ did and experienced. Through the Incarnation, whereby the Son of God became a man among human beings, all people enjoy a real degree of conformity to Christ, and to that extent a real measure of grace: nourished by this mystery, Christian faith has always joyfully confessed that all people are true brothers or sisters to Christ.

"Continuing" Incarnation

The conviction that all people are in an original state of grace is based on the concept of an Incarnation that is not only *redemptive* but also *continuing*—that is, that involves contemporaneity with the risen

Christ. The Incarnation is not simply a once-upon-a-time event; it is even now an ongoing reality. In our insistence on the grace-full union of all people with Christ through the Incarnation, we might seem to be neglecting the Resurrection—and clearly a theology of redemption that did not include it would be unbalanced and impoverished. Our omission, however, is only apparent; for at the heart of all we are saying is the conviction that the resurrection of Christ did not withdraw him from the human personal order. It did not make his humanity into something less human that might be illusory and ultimately unreal. By being taken up into the glory of God, Christ's human nature did not simply become a dead trophy or a mere accessory; rather it was given its hitherto unsuspected full human authenticity. Since the risen Lord is everlastingly assuming his glorified humanness, the Resurrection does not bring the Incarnation to a close, but continues it.

Even today, in his Eternal Now, Christ continues to assume his glorified body and humanness. The dynamic character of his continuing incarnation, which extends into Christ's glorification, is the foundation on which all grace is grounded. If Christ were not, even now, continually assuming his humanness, he would be little more for us than a memory, a paradigmatic individual of the past like Buddha, Socrates, or Gandhi, whose deeds and words, life and death, portray something compelling as examples to many of us. Grace would be meaningless babble if Christ were not still becoming incarnate. The truth and reality of grace lies precisely in the fact that the risen Lord continues to assume his human nature and, through it, the bond-in-being that exists between all people. All the saving benefits that accrue to us through the Incarnation now derive from and refer to the risen Lord. This is very important in the personalist understanding of grace, since union with Christ, at whatever level of the personal order, is necessarily a personal union with the Body-Person of the risen Savior.

Contemporaneity with Christ is of the essence of grace; it guarantees and gives meaning to Christ's "I am with you." While it is true that the glorification of Jesus by the Father has taken him from the visible horizon of human life, it has not taken him out of the human personal order. Traditional Catholic theology has not always taken this sufficiently into account. The failure to give serious consideration to the abiding, "contemporary" nature of the Lord's personal union with all people had the result that the doctrine concerning Christ was sometimes applied without qualification to the doctrine concerning the church. In that case, the dangers inherent in a false identification of the church with Christ could not be avoided. It seems to me that some Catholic teaching on the church as the Mystical Body went perilously far in this direction. Such an identification had an extremely misleading effect: Not only did the role and mission of the church seem to eclipse that of Christ, but the vision of the risen Christ standing in heaven making intercession for us almost passed out of sight. The idea of a "continuing" incarnation referred no longer to the essential fact that Christ is still actively assuming his glorified humanness; instead, the reference was to the continuing presence of Christ in the visible church. As Simone Weil said in her *Letter to a Priest:* "Everything has proceeded as though in the course of time no longer Jesus, but the church, had come to be regarded as being God incarnate on this earth."

Of course, the church is not the "extension" of the Incarnation if by that is meant (as is often the case) that it is Jesus Christ himself. It is *not* he himself but the church of which he is Head. The truly continuing Christ is the glorified and living Christ (who has at no time abdicated in favor of the church!). When the doctrinal balance is redressed, instead of the church being the center around which everything in the order of salvation must gravitate, the world, the church, and all people gravitate around the risen Lord. It is precisely because Christ is still directly and immediately caught up in the human personal order that he can and does draw all things to himself (John 12:32).

It should be quite clear that "once" given to all people, this saving union with Christ has a "for all" quality about it: It is not an isolated and ineffective union, but an abiding personal presence of Christ that actively involves all people. Thus the reality—and not just the possibility—of universal grace is established by the continuing "emergence" of the Lord in history and in the personal order of humankind. The advent of grace is always present in the hearts of all people. It is only because grace *is* there that people can become full participants in that which Christ is. It is only because people are already in such a radical state of grace, and hence united to Christ, that they are personally invited to appropriate this Christian kinship through active relations.

In the light of these preliminary yet important remarks, we shall now attempt to explore the personalist basis for an adequate account of universal grace. We must distinguish three specific levels of "being-together-with-others" in the personal order: (1) the deeper level of basic reciprocity, (2) the intermediate level of solidarity, and (3) the outward level of active personal relations. Universal grace stems from the fact that Christ is present and with us at each of these three strata of the personal order. In being made human he is enmeshed in the web of basic reciprocity that unites all people, caught up in the solidarity wherein people live and define themselves; and he freely enters into the world of human relations. It is precisely this anchorhold that the human personal order has on Christ that releases universal grace in and throughout the world. We shall examine these three strata of the personal order to see how thoroughly grounded and present Christ is in them.

Basic Reciprocity

Between all people there is a basic bond-in-being, a "reciprocity of existence," as it is sometimes called. This means that to speak of the person is not in the first instance to speak of individuals who somehow become related to other individuals, but to speak of people who from the start cannot have their personhood defined save in relation to other persons. Even prior to any conscious encounter with others, the human person neither stands alone nor can be defined alone. "Being" and "being related to" are but two essentially interdependent features of the same reality: the human person. Subjectivity cannot exist, still less be conceived, without intersubjectivity; they define and support one another. A human person is an individual "self" *because* it exists in reciprocity with others. Conversely, persons are related to one another *because* each exists as a self in its own right. We can illustrate something of this correlation with an example taken from common experience, namely, the relationship that defines "father" and "son" or again that which defines "husband" and "wife." In either instance, there is no priority of the relationship over its terms, nor of the terms over the relation. They are in fact reciprocal. Similarly, the basic reciprocity or bond-in-being between persons simultaneously places them one beside the other as well as one with another. We say that this reciprocity is basic or "primordial" because it defines the personal nature with which people begin to exist. It is not, as we have already indicated, something that we acquire by actively relating to other people. The collegial nature is a given fact that constitutes personhood as such. Humanity thus appears as a real, indissoluble totality of really related persons—a community of persons.

It is in this very real ontological sense that the person is said to be created in the image of the one and triune God. As the most perfect beings with personal existence, the Divine Persons exist only in relationship to one another. The reciprocity that unites and defines them as Persons is not somehow superadded to the unity of God's nature, but rather constitutes this very unity and is identical with it. So it is with human persons. The expression "made in the image of God" therefore not only indicates a task, a vocation, which people must strive to realize in their lifetime, but also denotes the given reality of their basic nature *as* persons.

The basic reciprocity that we are here describing gives humankind its most radical unity. As a spiritual reality, this bond-in-being transcends time and space and establishes a far deeper and more meaningful unity among people than does the mere fact of biological descent. It is, of course, true that the human race does constitute a unified whole on the

basis that a similar nature is passed on to all its
members from one generation to another. Important as this may be for the propagation of the spe-
cies, the real basis and justification of humankind's
unity lies in the basic reciprocity that binds all human beings in a transpersonal whole. What are
important for us here are the grace-full effects that
result from Christ's involvement in human reciprocity.

By making the decision to become a human being, the Son of God entered and became part of
human reciprocity; as an actual member of the human race he is himself caught up and bound to
every other member. Without having assumed a
human person as such, Christ nevertheless assumed everything that the human person is and
does, including reciprocity. He thus stands united
to every human person just as surely as all people,
by definition, are present to one another. The redemptive force of Christ's entry into the web of
human reciprocity constitutes an abiding funda-
ment of universal grace; indeed it is the central truth
of all grace. In this way, the actual state of humankind is radically transformed from within. Since
one member of the human race is the Son of God,
all the other members that exist within this same
reciprocity now refer to his divine Person. When
human beings come into existence, they are defined
at the deepest level of their personal existence by
this original relationship to Christ. To exist as a
human person is to be related and personally pre-

sent to *this* person who is Christ. Such is the realism with which Christ says to every person "I am with you." Such is the reality of original grace as it exists in the heart of everyone.

Human reciprocity establishes all people in Christ; it also differentiates them from the Son of God and, indeed, from one another in their onto-logical "otherness." Yet it is sufficient that one member of the human race should be elevated and united to God in unity of person in order to engrace all people. Together they exist in a bond-in-being which in Christ now unites them to God the Father and to one another in the Holy Spirit. It is with this profound sense of achievement that Christ prayed to his heavenly Father: "I have bestowed on them the glory you have bestowed on me, that they may be one as we are one—I in them and you in me. Thus their oneness will be perfected" (John 17:22). For when Christ laid hold of a portion of human existence for his saving mission, he assumed the basic reciprocity that binds all people to one another and to himself. This personal "contact" which all people enjoy with Christ is the foundation of uni-versal grace. We thus rediscover on a personalist basis the constant assertion of Christian tradition that the Incarnation has a grace-full effect on every member of the human family and that divine grace is given not merely *for* but *to* all people.

It thus stands to reason that it is not enough to say that by Christ's life, death, and resurrection we are saved "in principle" —as though Christ's entry into the personal world of human beings had only touched and affected human nature in general, that is, abstracting from the individual person who makes up the human family. For the fact is that every person who is called into being is engraced by Christ. This state of original grace—a possession that we have as the abiding consequence of God's incarnate love and that possesses us in our inmost being—is the ground and justification of all subsequent transformations that occur in the order of grace. One such transformation, which we shall now examine more closely, takes place on the second level of the personal order, that is, the intermediate level of personal solidarity.

Personal Solidarity

Thus far we have considered the foundation of universal grace and have said almost nothing about its dynamic character. The reason is that it discloses its dynamic and active presence principally through the bond of personal solidarity uniting all people. Like the human personal order from which it emerges, universal grace calls forth and engages human powers. It is not only *present:* it is *at work* among people. How this is so will become clear as we see just what personal solidarity involves and how it is radically transformed by Christ's presence.

First, it is important to distinguish between what is commonly understood by human solidarity and what we mean here by "personal solidarity." Human solidarity is generally taken to mean that feeling of mutual dependence that arises between people as a result of working and living together. Clearly, those involved in a common task or bent on the execution of a specific project do indeed develop strong fellow feelings and a community of interests, purposes, and actions. Sociologists have cataloged many such forms of fraternities, associations, fellowships, and unions. They often exemplify the functional nature of society. In the functional society, I seek the other and the other seeks me with a view to attaining together an external common goal. Either of us, therefore, could be replaced by some third person if that person had the same capacities as the one for whom he or she was substituting. Human solidarity subsists in the conditioned and efficient responses people give to the demands made on them by others. Even in a community not necessarily aimed at providing for a need or remedying a deficiency, the solidarity that comes to exist between its members is the result of active relationships. Although people get together more for reasons of conviviality than for collaboration, the solidarity between them is nonetheless the direct result of having come and lived together.

Personal solidarity, on the other hand, exists prior to any personal or collective activity whatsoever; it exists as a bond between people even before they meet or congregate. Before I actually confront another person, before I even have the chance to say hello, a bond of personal solidarity unites us. Whether we fully realize it or not, this pre-given solidarity and oneness makes us "soul brothers." Within the personal order, this personal solidarity lies halfway between basic reciprocity, on the one hand, and active "I-thou" relations, on the other. It hinges on both, as we shall see, while remaining distinct from either.

The distinguishing characteristic of this solidarity is that it challenges and induces a person to take an active stand or position in the face of others. It is not the response itself, but the inducement to respond —that inner summons which elicits from the individual a free response in the face of others. Because people are fundamentally united in personal solidarity, they necessarily implicate one another in everything they think, will, and do. It is precisely this involuntary yet unavoidable involvement in the lives and actions of others that evokes a reaction in the individual person, eliciting a personal response of acceptance or rejection. What the other does or becomes is my responsibility because we are soul brothers, and so it has power to incriminate me. Thus this pre-given solidarity invariably prompts me to redefine myself and my position in the light of what the other person does or becomes. At this level of personal existence, there can be no spiritual indifference or neutrality.

Is it not true that when we are confronted with someone who is a stranger it is impossible for us to look upon that person in complete detachment, with indifference? This other person, the "thou," enters our life either as a friend or as a foe, a gift or a threat. Even before the walls of our self-composure break down, even before our feelings of sympathy or antipathy are aroused, even before we consciously decide to align ourselves with or against him, we have either offered ourself to him or have found it necessary to withhold the offer. We can never look at any person without a sense of our pre-given solidarity because it is other people who make us our "self." Interpersonal dynamics of this kind can only mean that a bond of solidarity between people exists which is of the essence of personhood.

Although personal solidarity exists, as we have seen, prior to any active relations between persons, it manifests itself most clearly in those acts whereby we press one another into taking a stand, whether positive or negative, vis-à-vis one another. In fact, personal reactions of any kind—whether acquiescence or protest—disclose something of this pre-existing bond of solidarity between people. It is this very bond that invariably elicits from people a personal commitment and response of some kind. However, a most striking manifestation of the bond of solidarity is seen in those acts whereby people try to disengage their responsibility from a situation through acts of revolt.

In every typical rebellious act, the one who revolts engages in an action that is essentially aimed at dissociating himself from other persons. Through his act of revolt, the rebel desperately attempts to disengage his personal responsibility. The reason he feels compelled to do so is that personal solidarity has placed him before a *fait accompli:* prior to his own free choice he finds himself unwittingly implicated in the personal acts and purposes of others. In other words, it gradually dawns on him that he has become of necessity an accomplice. Before his insurrection, he may or may not be fully aware of this association in guilt; yet the existing bond of solidarity has already incriminated him and will soon elicit from him a conscious stand over against the others. When this happens, he ruthlessly disengages his personal responsibility by revolting. Initially, every act of revolt or protest marks a deliberate attempt to break solidarity with those one considers blameworthy.

The general observations concerning the nature and dynamics of solidarity should help us to reach a better understanding of the deeper implications of Christ's intimate involvement in our personal existence. As we have already pointed out, the Incarnation is not simply an event of the past, but an enduring condition of the present. This means in the reality of the Incarnation Christ is still with us; even now he stands person-to-person with us in personal solidarity. Redemption is rightly described as Christ's sharing in the lot of sinners and suffering the death that is theirs. He redeems humankind by really identifying himself with the sinner. As St. Paul says, he assumed the "flesh of sin" (Rom. 8:3). "For our sake God made the sinless one into sin" (2 Cor. 5:21). He, the innocent one without sin, becomes humiliatingly incriminated in the sin and guilt of humankind. Personal solidarity places Christ in a situation of guilt, and he is summoned from within to take an active stand with regard to the acts of people, including their sinful acts. Through his absolute refusal to yield to the subjugating force of sin, he is able to tip the balance of personal solidarity in our favor and radically reverse its hitherto irresistible attraction toward evil. It is a breakthrough in personal solidarity that is to have grace-full repercussions in the hearts of all people. We call the hidden reality—which is ever present and silently at work in the world—universal grace.

It is difficult to conceive of the revulsion and anguish that Christ must have experienced as a result of his personal solidarity with people in our sin. His pure conscience was certainly in constant revolt against sinful acts, inwardly repudiating them and dissociating itself from all personal responsibility and guilt. In his innermost being, Christ must have been, above all, a "conscientious objector"—a definition that perhaps gives us our best insight into the character of Jesus of Nazareth. Having implicated Christ so inescapably in our sinful situation, this very same solidarity elicited from him that absolutely unique response, completely unexpected, which resounds in history: Under no condition would he become an accomplice in sin; he freely accepts the final defeat—death—rather than to compromise. To the end on the cross, Christ defies the evil sway of human solidarity. He not only consents to die, but accepts death as a consequence of his defiance. Committing himself completely, he holds nothing in reserve.

The freedom that we see above all illustrated in the life of Christ consists in being so totally dedicated to the good that evil has lost its power to attract. Through the exercise of such freedom, Christ was able to free all people. The mystery concerning the divine and human elements in the Son of God is irreducible, but as a human being Christ was certainly vulnerable; Scripture records his tempting. Yet he was able to endure the full force of this evil sway without making the slightest concession to it. Confronted by evil, his innocent conscience was concentrated in a radical refusal. Christian tradition has always seen endurance and fortitude as the hallmark of Christ's earthly life and as that which, more than anything else, changed humankind's condition for the better. Christ's endurance was the ultimately decisive test of active fortitude: None of the injuries he suffered, even up to death, ever deflected him from his course of love; he suffered without hatred or any thought of vengeance. This will always remain the definitive criterion in judging the morality of violence, namely, the presence or absence of hatred, bitterness, and desire for revenge in the heart of the rebel. I think it may well be the only valid reason why the use of violence can never by sanctioned by Christians. Since the truth and reality of grace are to be sought in the person of Christ, the only justifiable form of Christian witness is a life of endurance in peace, justice, and love. The violence inflicted on Christ puts him, so to speak, in a position beyond violence, makes him a totally nonviolent person because he went through violence without being contaminated by it.

This "superhuman" stance in the face of evil becomes an authentic *repeatable* possibility for us as the outcome of our redemption. The principal saving effect of Christ's revolt was the breakthrough we have spoken of that produced a fundamental change in the bond of solidarity between people. Instead of being compromised or dominated by evil, the human person could now dominate it. The contagious, irreversible trend toward perversion and corruption that was leading humankind to destruction is checked and reversed in Christ. His entire saintly life, and particularly his death, which expresses in one and the same last breath supreme renunciation and supreme charity, now become a personal situation in which all people are involved and one with which every person must reckon.

Universal grace is thus both present and at work in the personal order. Slowly but surely, it reduces the would-be alternatives open to us until finally we are unable and unwilling to remain spiritually neutral or indifferent. Grace summons us from within and elicits a free decision. We must choose. It is as though somewhere in the depths of our personal being and conscience, we hear the words

"He who is not with me is against me" (Matt. 12:30).
Should we remain indifferent, we have by that very
fact already committed ourselves to a responsible
decision of rejection. Not to respond at all or to
choose indifference is already a personal commitment. In real life, therefore, people are either sinners breaking solidarity with Christ or just people
who are promoting their solidarity with Christ. The
sheer inescapability of such a basic option is the
work of universal grace.

The grace of our solidarity with Christ must be
seen, first of all, as removing the possibility of remaining neutral. It is precisely in removing our
self-destructive neutrality and in eliciting from us a
free decision for Christ that universal grace discloses itself as a truly dynamic reality. It liberates our
freedom for Christ, a freedom we could not know
save by the grace of God's redemptive Incarnation.
This does not mean that choice is made any easier,
or that it does not carry an enormous responsibility.
As we have already seen, such is the personal solidarity among people that when we make a personal
choice we are choosing, not merely for ourselves,
but for all people. In the act of choice we are not
simply saying, "This is what I choose for myself,"
but also "This is what everyone must choose." By
my existence, by what I become through my choice,
I am determining what all humankind everywhere
is forever to become. One cannot bear the burden of
such responsibility for all without experiencing
"anguish." This is the reason Kierkegaard says we

choose only "in fear and trembling" and why he speaks of the "dizziness of freedom." Nevertheless, universal grace gives us values for which we are willing to assume freely what would otherwise be a crushing responsibility. Given humankind's solidarity with Christ, individuals are no longer "condemned" to be free; we are free to be free. Our freedom is liberated for Christ and everything that Christ stands for. It is at bottom the freedom to love one's neighbor as Christ has loved us—without reserve or calculation, utterly and completely. Love and love alone can consistently be willed for all and by all.

Nowhere is the primacy of God's love asserted more realistically and more universally than in the redemptive Incarnation that unites all people to Christ in a radical bond of solidarity, a state of original grace, and that touches and affects all people from within. In Christ the personal order is infused with grace. The contacts spread out deep in all directions, reaching even to the ends of the earth. We can recognize them, but can follow them only so far and no farther. In the end they withdraw into a core of mystery where our gaze cannot penetrate. Unseen and unspoken, the reality of Christ's "I am with you" is silently at home in the hearts of all people.

3

"You Are My Friends"

If Christian existence sinks its roots into the deeper reaches of the personal order and takes its real origin in the hidden depths of our being, where Christ is already present to us, it nevertheless surfaces into the broad daylight of a living friendship with Christ. This new emergence of grace, which characterizes Christian life, is not simply the disclosure or unveiling of something that had always been present though hidden. It cannot be compared to the exposed tip of an iceberg that merely suggests the hidden mass of ice underneath it, or to the eruption of hot lava that suddenly issues forth from the bowels of an active volcano. Certainly it is that, but much more. More than the epiphany of a hitherto undisclosed grace, Christian existence inaugurates the creation of a startlingly new reality: a bond of friendship with Christ. It is necessary now to take a searching and serious look at this unprecedented bond.

Every authentic life has a ground of its own from which it springs and from which it is never severed.

Christian life is no exception. The foundation on which Christians know themselves to be grounded is nothing less than Christ's personal friendship. At this highest, most intimate level of the personal order, Christ not only says "I am with you," as he does to all people, but to some he also says "You are my friends." In personalist terms, the difference between these two simple statements marks all the difference between the grace of non-Christians and that of Christians. The first and last word that can ever be said of Christian life is that it exists whenever and wherever Christ strikes up an authentic friendship with human beings. From the viewpoint of intimacy with God, such a friendship was already foreshadowed in the Old Testament. The supreme revelation of Yahweh to Moses on Sinai was as intimate as a person speaking face to face to a friend (Exod. 33:15). Only to friends does one reveal one's innermost thoughts and secrets. Hence Jesus says to his disciples: "I have called you friends, because all that I have heard from my Father I have made known to you" (John 15:15). To the disciples, Jesus is a "friend," one who naturally confides his hopes and purposes to those he loves. Thus, initiated into the secrets of the Lord, the Christian disciples feel themselves summoned to all the other privileges as well as to the duties of true friends. They are drawn into the intimacy and strength of that community whose only ground for being is Christ's "You are my friends."

When we recall the properties and the high demands of authentic friendship and reflect, further, that it is only on the Lord's initiative that people are called to such an intimate fellowship with him, we begin to realize the truly remarkable and transcendent quality of Christian life. Unlike the domain of mere human friendship, where either partner may initiate the friendly relationship, Christians do not suppose for a moment that friendship with Christ is of their own making; that in some way they have by their own choosing or wisdom placed themselves in the privileged position they occupy. On the contrary, when Christ befriends this or that person, he does so by a free selection and knows no other necessity than the freedom of his divine love. It is not that some people "happen upon" or "come across" Jesus Christ and that seeing or hearing of him their hearts break away, run to him and cling to him; rather Christ comes to them, turns and looks upon them, and says: "I choose you as my friends."

Typical of Christ's radical initiative in choosing his friends is the gospel account of his encounter with the rich young man. Mark notes with enigmatic brevity: "And Jesus fixing his eyes upon him loved him" (10:21). We can discern here an inward impulse of admiring affection that makes the first advance. Jesus felt instinctively drawn to this clean, earnest character. He alone determines just who his friends will be. The interesting, beautiful, splendid aspect of this friendship when the choice is made is that it always comes as a surprise, an unexpected discovery. It can never really be planned in advance; it is a surprise gift, as it was for the rich young man.

This gospel episode highlights yet another important truth about friendship with Christ that cannot be overlooked: the possibility of refusing to respond to his loving advances. The rich young man rejects intimate fellowship with Christ in the fullest personal freedom. Gloom fell upon his face, we are told, and he went away sorrowful. It is quite clear that although Christ takes the sole initiative in determining who his real friends will be, such a friendship can materialize only if the other person reciprocates. Both persons must freely and spontaneously will the same thing: mutual promotion. Hence the surprise of authentic friendship can come only as a mutual surprise, a surprise that consists in the sudden evidence of a perfect and genuine reciprocity. In the domain of friendship nothing can be extorted—not even by divine love.

In the heightened intimacy of friendship, a new bond is created between Christ and the individual and a new life is begun. Christian life finds its essential and basic meaning in this new bond which gives two friends access to the unique world of the "other" and issues in active relationships of faith, hope, and love. Friendship shows its true face in these three types of relationship, which can be defined more basically as communication, mutual support, and communion, respectively. Our next step, therefore, will be to examine each of these essential aspects of friendship. When the true countenance of friendship emerges more clearly, we will be able to see how our considerations, when applied to Christian life, not only retain their full validity but also gain an unsuspected depth and transcendence.

Communication and Faith

Real friendship consists first in a frank, unhesitating opening of one's heart and mind to the other; it is the altogether free and independent communication of one's own person. Hence it allows the other to see right in and know us as we really are, unstintingly sharing what we ourselves are and have learned.

This is possible only if there is a willingness to communicate on both sides. That is where many an acquaintance falls short of friendship. It is quite possible that we have come across someone dozens of times, even talked occasionally, without ever really encountering that person. Not all forms of communication are truly personal. From acquaintances, as opposed to real friends, we can part without any feeling of separation or any great desire of seeing each other again. In contrast to this indifference, we need only recall the great sense of loss and separation the disciples of Jesus experienced when their Friend was about to take leave of them. Personal communication of this high order is essentially an encounter that renders the believing partners accessible to each other in their inward aspect.

Furthermore, the openness of friendship calls for the total disarmament belonging to faith. Encounters in friendship are necessarily encounters without weapons. Between friends, there can be no built-in reservations, mental restrictions, or time limits. Only in total vulnerability can believing partners reveal themselves to one another in perfect availability and friendship. They must encounter one another not *despite* their human defects, but simply *with* their defects, because these happen to be part of the friend's makeup and nature. This explains why the surrender and faith of friendship mark a summit in personal communication. Here we need only recall the living language of faith to recognize this unique quality of friendship. Faith is commonly described as "absolute confidence in . . . " or "unconditional acceptance of. . ." or "trust without guarantee. . . ." Such a complete and total surrender is essential to authentic friendship.

Yet Christian faith transcends human friendship in at least two remarkable ways. First, it supposes that Christ is still very much alive today and therefore capable of striking up an "I-thou" relationship of personal communication and friendship with us. A pale analogy of this occurs on the purely human level when a person continues to believe in a dear friend who has died and yet nevertheless remains invisibly, if mysteriously, present. Indeed, it is not uncommon that when a close friend dies, we find that our friend somehow becomes even more present to us than formerly. We come to think of him or her not as someone who has passed away, but as a continuing inspiration. This mysterious presence of the dead within the community of the living is a theme that is prevalent in all religious systems. However, the post mortem fellowship that Christians experience with Jesus Christ is of an entirely different order. The reason for this difference is that Christ is not dead, but risen and remarkably alive. The blessed certainty of this fundamental truth comes only with the surrender and risk of faith. In the realm of personal realities there can be no real "proof." As a personal reality—and indeed in a definitive sense—the risen Christ can only be encountered when people are ready to open themselves to the message of the resurrection and to take the risk of letting their lives be determined by this good news. The one who takes this risk fearlessly and happily bears witness to Christ the Son of the living God. In fact, the death of Jesus becomes the consecration of Christian life itself: "Happy are those who have not seen and yet believe" (John 20:29).

The second truly unique characteristic about any personal communication with Christ is, as we have seen, that he alone can initiate the dialogue. We cannot communicate with Christ personally unless he first speaks to us. It is Christ's movement to us, above all his movement in us, that wins from us our obedient response to faith. Such need not be the case in ordinary human communication where any person can and often does initiate the conversation. Is not every spoken word, in effect, a call to some reaction, an invitation to some response? When we make a promise to someone, for example, are we not in fact seeking to elicit from that person the response of hope? Or when we testify in the presence of someone, are we not basically appealing for the response of trust? Personal communication with Christ is quite another thing. Not only must Christ dispatch the invitation, but in a mysteriously efficacious way he alone can call into being our believing response. Thus the inherent power of Christ's communication promotes a person to the state of a "believing person," a "responding partner." His grace penetrates to the most intimate core of our personal freedom and activates an exchange that issues in face-to-face dialogue with a human partner who will respond with the peculiar faithfulness typical of authentic friendship. Yet this personal bond of friendship struck up between Christ and the individual is by no means exhausted in faith alone. While faith undoubtedly marks an essential element in this friendship and continues as its enduring source, something more is required— mutual support and hope carrying this union to even greater heights of intimacy and durability.

Mutual Support and Hope

In every real friendship there is trust—believing in the other, counting on him, never doubting his loyalty or support but looking toward the future with him in confidence. The rise from communication to mutual support, from faith to hope, marks a new register of intimacy between friends. Whereas faith sets partners face-to-face, mutual support or hope places them side-by-side. This new engagement enables them to shoulder one another's burdens in their united striving to face the future that they themselves must create and bring about. This new state of personal affairs is what we call "hope."

Hope is an essential feature of human existence generally, and of friendship in particular. Without hope there can be no true friends. Hopeful partners are so intimately united that one cannot let the other down without at the same time totally betraying himself and breaking the engagement on which the other has placed all his hopes. When I say to a friend, "You can count on me," I do not restrict "you" to any aspect or part of his being; I embrace him in his entire being. As we can see, this personal involvement is much more than the intermittent and often capricious relationship of companionship, helpfulness, and obligingness; it is a permanent union in which two partners sustain one another and are at each other's abiding and resourceful disposal. Over and above the determination of common interest and reasonable expectation, they discover one another as unique personal subjects. They do not draw their hope from each other's human possibilities, talents, and qualities, as though they were somehow reading the future in them. It is not the possibilities in the other that engender hope; rather it is hope that creates new possibilities and a new future for mutually helpful partners.

Though it is evident that we must move with caution in applying all this to a friendship in which one of the partners is the risen Christ, certain essentials remain. We have the witness of the saints that it is possible to think of the relation between Our Lord and his friends on the earth as a partnership in which the Christian collaborates in bringing to completion the work Christ began during his earthly life. For though God's promises to humankind have been confirmed and validated in Christ, they have not yet been fulfilled. There is mystery here that transcends our understanding; yet it seems quite evident that as Christ keeps his promise to be with us till the end of time, so our loyal friendship contributes to his work of redemption that is to come to its final achievement in the Last Days.

Having made these necessary distinctions, it is now possible to discuss Christian hope from the point of view from which we have been seeing it. It promotes Christ and the believer as resourceful partners. This mutual promotion, which for Christ constitutes the help he personally wants to be for us, elicits the active reliance of the believer, who finds new strength in Christ's own power and grace. Christian hope thus conjoins the believer and Christ in a partnership full of fresh possibilities, one in which they can advance toward their future together. We say "their" future advisedly, since it is

one that Christ and the Christian must bring about
together if this union in hope is to mature and reach
fulfillment.

Christian hope opens up an entirely unexpected
future for us, the real possibility of co-operating
personally with Christ in the work of salvation that
is to bring about a New Heaven and a New Earth.
People of hope do not simply stand waiting, antici-
pating a transformation of the world by God in the
ultimate future; rather, they move toward it, sharing in the process of transformation that is bringing
it about. What this future holds in store for Christ as
well as for his friends and the world cannot be fully
known until it comes about in the total newness of a
real creation. Yet even now it must urgently be
hoped for, since it has already been promised by
God. Through hope, the power of Christ becomes
the strength of Christians in their striving to bring
about the coming of the kingdom together. In this
respect, hope goes beyond faith without, however,
leaving it behind. It outstrips faith by establishing
itself in a creative partnership with Christ. Yet even
this partnership is not supreme, for in hope love
has the primacy. Hope prevails in love since "love
hopes all things" (1 Cor. 13:7).

Communion and Love

True friendship exists only between those who love
one another; it culminates in a willingness to spend
oneself for the other—and this not only ungrudg-

ingly, without reckoning the cost, but eagerly; indeed, one will give one's life if need be. "Greater love hath no man than this, that a man lay down his life for his friends" (John 15:13). The understanding of charity as friendship, and therefore first of all the pursuit of friendship, is basic to Christian life.

Over and above the dialogue of faith and the mutual support of hope, friendship attains a maximum of reciprocity in a loving communion. Love alone unites friends to the extent that they share one another's existence completely and wholeheartedly. In loving friendship the element of self-giving finds its deepest expression, since the gift that is given is ultimately always the givers themselves. It is at once the gift of personal being and the gift of being truly personal. More than any other interpersonal relationship, love reaches and transfigures the center of those who are loved. Not only do such people come to possess themselves more authentically, but the uniqueness of their person is given its hitherto undisclosed real value. At this level friendship attains a degree of spiritual intimacy that suspends, as it were, the laws of matter, surpasses our conception of time and space, and passes through the closed doors of corporeality and human opaqueness. A new sphere of existence is created and something quite unique takes place: the free self-giving of one person to another.

Christian existence follows the same pattern, opens the same doors, and creates its own eternity. Yet the pattern, the doors, and the eternity of friendship with Christ are entirely different. Christian love transcends human love in every way. Whether looking up from below, from the human point of view, or looking down from above as it were through the eyes of God, one cannot fail to be struck by the fact that intimate friendship with God defies the human "logic" of love. In the first place, friendship with Christ is so unexpected, unpredictable, and so extraordinarily unlikely. There is always that strange uncertainty as to why Christ calls one human being to intimacy with himself, and not another. Although something of the same mystery exists in human friendships, with Christ it borders on divine folly and utter absurdity. Nor can the mystery be explained away by the somewhat arbitrary fact of being born into a Christian home, or by the lucky accident of hearing about Christ through the word that the church preaches. Neither one of these factors can be excluded, yet neither adequately explains why Christ befriends *this* individual rather than *that* one.

The second surprising aspect of this friendship with Christ is that even the most insignificant individual becomes a significant, loving partner to Christ. The gospels provide ample evidence that the circle of loving friends that gradually grew up around Jesus was made up largely of very ordinary people—indeed people who were, if anything, conspicuously insignificant and uncomely by worldly standards. Jesus became the friend of the oppressed, the poor, and the abandoned; of those without legal rights and of those who were the victims of sin and injustice. Friendship with these, the "least of his brethren," was the hallmark of his loving kindness. The call of friendship went typically to Levi, the publican, a despicable sinner living outside the religious circles of God's people in uncleanness and disobedience. Jesus was often severely criticized about the company he kept and was dubbed by his critics "a friend of publicans and sinners" (Matt. 11:19). One has the strange impression that it was these who were most deeply initiated into the mysteries of Jesus' life and who in turn showed him the most love and understanding.

A third remarkable feature, and one that perhaps best distinguishes friendship with Christ from any other, is that it is not as rare as might be supposed. Humanly speaking, a true friend is a rare treasure and it is very doubtful whether one person can have several friends simultaneously. It is, of course, possible to have several friends, but the question is whether they all share one and the same friendship, whether there can really be an authentic "group of friends" in which all are immediately united in the same bond of friendship. Theoretically, there is no limit to what Aristotle calls *poluphilia* (many-friendedness). In practice, however, the possibility is severely limited by the time and place of one's personal presence. We all know from experience how difficult it is to maintain an intense bond of friendship with someone who, for long periods of time, lives hundreds of miles away. The proverbial "out of sight, out of mind" bespeaks more truth than we are generally prepared to admit. An even more formidable obstacle to many-friendedness stems from the nature and high demands of friendship itself. When a personal relationship is carried to its highest peak of intensity, as it invariably must be in real friendship, its extension is limited beyond all telling by the demands of increased intimacy.

Christian existence, which we have defined as personal friendship with Christ, transcends these two human limitations. No distance, geographical or psychological, separates the risen Lord from his friends on earth. His passage into the eternity of the Father is not a turning away or an alienation from earth, nor is his ascension into glory the kind of rootlessness that would leave his friends far below and without personal contact with him. Rather, the risen Lord gains an unprecedented creative presence more universal and interior to us than he could ever have known by remaining visibly present on earth. Thus, the number of personal friends he can have on earth is as unlimited as the universal extension of his altogether new and enduring presence. And, what is more, be his friends as numerous as the grains of sand on earth or as widely scattered abroad as the stars in the heavens, he can still love each one of them personally as if each were his only friend on earth. This undivided attention and love that Christ lavishes on each of his friends in no way splinters or fragments his wider circle of friends. On the contrary, what is given to one is never taken away from another; it cements and holds the Christian "group of friends" together ever more permanently in the same friendship. This incomprehensible yet familiar cohesive power of Christ's loving friendship is creative of a new corporate life that is called the church.

Through faith, hope, and love Christ promotes his friends to a truly "catholic" state that constitutes the very essence of the church. Faith in Christ not only promotes believers individually and privately, but establishes them in a community of believers. Christian hope is also communal. By raising up believers to active partnership with himself in the work of salvation, Christ thereby entrusts his friends to one another. In so doing, he builds up a vast concert of mutually helpful partners who are shoulder to shoulder in their drive to reach and take hold of his promised future. This ecclesial dimension is given ultimate reality and depth of expression in the love that Christians have for one another. The church thus becomes a *corpus caritatis*, a loving whole, in which Christ's friends love one another even as he loves them. His love for them becomes the ground and motive of their love. By this sign all people will know that they are his disciples—by cherishing love for one another (John 13:35).

From what we have been saying it is clear that authentic friendship with Christ necessarily takes on a public form and assumes social consequences. Christ does not befriend us as isolated individuals without any mutual bonds, but as members of a single people, a church, whose essential reality is rooted in the unity of his loving friendship. In this sense, the church does more than make official a reality already duly established: It consecrates, promotes, sustains, and eventually protects this loving relationship and in so doing modifies its impact profoundly. Life in the church is then experienced as an avowal of one's positive response to Christ and as a request to the Christian community to nourish, strengthen, and deepen this response.

Outside the church, there is indeed grace and the possibility of personally encountering the risen Christ. The slightest heartfelt impulse toward one's neighbor is already an assimilation of the mind and life of Christ, and as such is not altogether unrelated to the church's own existence. But what is not possible or conceivable outside the divine milieu and circle of Christ's intimate friends is a lifelong, enduring, and intense fellowship with Christ. It is one thing to encounter Christ on one or other occasion, like the two blind men in the gospel, or to touch the hem of his garment like the woman with a hemorrhage, and quite another thing to live constantly and intimately with him as did the twelve apostles. In the former, the presence of the Lord meant a sudden flash of recognition, utterly convincing but soon over. What the woman with a hemorrhage, for example, had relied on for release from her affliction was the one thing that people are meant to rely on for release from all their afflictions, namely the life and work of Jesus recognized as the saving power of God active in the world. She thus becomes a model for those who want to enter into relationship with Jesus and win from him the affectionate address "Son" or "Daughter." On the whole, however, all such encounters were sporadic, elusive, and in the end evanescent. Although they did not prove permanent, they left in the minds of those to whom they happened an unshakable conviction that they had, for a short period of time at least, been in the direct presence of their living Savior.

During Jesus' ministry on earth there were also people who constantly followed him. Much of this was a spontaneous enthusiasm for his words and deeds; much of it also was simple curiosity seeking. But there were a chosen few who followed him as a vocation; they had heard his call of friendship and responded to it by "clinging" to his person in an enduring relationship. This was most certainly true of the inner group that drew together around Jesus: the Twelve. It consisted of men who were wholly committed to Jesus, who had left all to put themselves at his disposal. Commitment to him, they soon learned, meant even more than leaving home and livelihood. "If anyone comes to me and does not hate his father and mother, wife and children, brothers and sisters, even his own life, he cannot be a disciple of mine. No one who does not carry his cross and come with me can be a disciple of mine" (Luke 14:26–27).

It is no accident that such a protracted personal contact with Christ was the only criterion used by the primitive church to fill the vacancy left by Judas (Acts 1:21–22). Eligible for service as an apostle were those who had maintained a close connection with Jesus from the time of John the Baptist's ministry until Jesus' ascension, and consequently could bear witness to his resurrection. Such a rigorous demand was not only a precondition for apostleship, but the basic feature of true friendship with Christ. Mark explicitly mentions the fact that when Jesus called the Twelve, he appointed them to be "with him" (3:14), the purpose being for them to enjoy close fellowship with him. In fact this call was to mark the beginning of their sharing life together, the beginning of close friendship. From this point on Jesus would address them thus: "To you my friends I say. . . " (Luke 12:4). They were now in Jesus and he in them; they could exchange places with him as only real friends can: "He who receives you receives me" (Matt. 10:40). "He who hears you hears me, and he who rejects you rejects me" (Luke 10:16).

For the Christian, the sign of this personal identification is baptism, through which the foundation and durability of friendship with Christ is guaranteed. In all the provisional things of the world nothing except the rejection of that friendship can separate us from Christ. In this connection it is most revealing that the gospels do not tell us that the twelve apostles had to be baptized. Yet great emphasis is placed on Paul's baptism, notwithstanding his brief and dramatic encounter with the risen Lord. We see here, as the early fathers of the church suggested, that the privilege of living in undivided intimacy with Jesus must have conferred on the Twelve the compendious grace of baptism. Considering the great prominence given to the baptismal rite in the history of the Christian church, it is rather surprising to note how seldom this important close association is referred to directly.

Clearly, a person cannot enjoy real friendship with Christ unless prepared to share his way and personal existence. "Following Jesus," as the New Testament uses the expression, means a complete fellowship and association with him, living with him and also suffering with him. It means, above all, being led into an intimate life-giving friendship with him and a total commitment to the program of his kingdom. The uniqueness of this living friendship becomes fully evident by noting its implications and results. On the one hand, Christ is there to show the *way* to all his friends. On the other hand, the *strength* to follow him also arises out of this friendship. To his friends, Christ has two hands, as it were: one to point out the way (*exemplum*) and the other to strengthen and help them onward (*sacramentum*). This dual aspect of the believer's union with Christ has always been regarded as the twofold basis of all Christian life.

As the pattern of Christian life, Jesus Christ indicates a definite way of life into which his friends are called, caught up, and assimilated. It is "his " way of life and no other, hence a particular way of self-giving, cross-bearing, self-denial, humiliation, and suffering; a particular way, that is, of serving and loving one's neighbor. Nor was this to be any vague and formless sort of love. Rather it must be Christ's own brand of love, the "way" he truly loved people, with all the constants that unmistakably characterize his loving kindness. Like Christ, the Christian must love in the form of "heartfelt mercy," "kind receptive openness," "readiness to serve," "meekness that does not defend itself," "long-suffering patience"—in short, a love like Christ's that can endure one's unendurable neighbor, forgive unpardonable sins, and love unlovable people.

Yet, Christ is not only the pattern and norm of his friends' lives; he is also their inner strength. The example of Christ's life becomes possible only to those with whom he has established an enduring bond of friendship. Only then can his "way" be urged on them with any real hope of conformity. Without the new life that personal friendship with Christ brings people and the new powers that it accords them, Christian life would be simply a futile kind of "yoga of self-endeavor" (Tinsley), a vain attempt to copy the external pattern of a good life through one's own effort and struggle. However, Christian life is of an entirely different order. It not only shows Christians what they are called to be, but enables them to be it. The intrinsic reality of Christ's church is precisely that new life that people receive through personal friendship with Christ.

If the necessary form and substance of Christian life lies in faith, hope, and charity, its essential context is the community of Christ's intimate friends. The center of this community is clearly defined: It is Jesus and those closest to him. The Christian church is above all the central place, the heart and context, where friendship with Christ has its roots, is given firmer and steadier bonds, blossoms and reaches full maturity. It is the natural womb out of which this friendship is born, just as the human being is born in the bosom of the family. There in the church its elementary needs are met, and only there will it ever feel completely "at home." Only in the ecclesial context are the occasions of meeting Christ on a sustained person-to-person basis adequately provided and sufficiently guaranteed. Outside the church (yet who can say exactly where its boundaries are drawn or its influence felt?) friendship with Christ, however promising, is deprived of the living and life-giving support of community; and it is within the community that the person is saved.

Authentic friendship with Christ is preserved from withering away and dying only when it can pulsate within the community of his intimate friends. In this important respect, the Christian church is like the human heart whose function it is to give unity to our diversity. All that we are and do unfolds from his vital organ. The human heart is that ultimate ground of our being wherein everything about us and in us is tied together and fastened centrally. Our whole "bloodstream," every path of our personal life, runs into the heart, in order to go out again from it. As it is with the human heart, so it is with the church. Christians can say, will, and do nothing that does not spring from this ecclesial center in which alone their whole being is established in the unity of Christ's loving friendship. Our whole Christian life unfolds and circulates from this vital source. In a personal sense, all else is empty, insubstantial, and unreal.

PART TWO

UNIVERSAL GRACE TAKEN SERIOUSLY

4

Christians and Non-Christians

If universal grace is taken seriously, it quickly becomes apparent that God never does things in a small, miserly way, but always with a reckless abandon and lavishness characteristic of infinite love. The intrinsic reality of universal grace is that God is forever letting his love get out of hand, out of his hands and into ours. Whether this happens when Christ says "You are my friends" (as he does to Christians), or when he says "I am with you" (as he does to all people), his grace touches and affects everyone. It is present everywhere in the world as a pulse of that Christ-life that brings the whole of creation and humanity's obstinate upward struggle toward God, ending in God, and finding its guiding lines in the divine life.

In view of our insistence on the truly universal character of divine grace, the reader may wonder if there is any real difference after all between Christians and non-Christians, between believers and non-believers, and if so, just what this difference is. With Christ's active presence in both, can this difference be characterized as one of degree or of kind? At first glance, this may appear as an abstract or purely theoretical question. In fact, it is one that the present-day situation throws up with urgency. Can Christians today, for all the intents and purposes of God's kingdom, truly rely on the grace of their secular neighbors? Must they recognize it as being basically akin to their own, and consequently as the genuine basis of a "wider ecumenism"? Can they subscribe unconditionally to the positive human values that are being realized in the world of unbelief? Can they safely accept as God's design the fact that his church is, and must remain, a minority church in a pluralistic world society?

Without wishing to imply that any simple answer to these questions can be adequate, I should like to urge that any substantial answer will have to take universal grace seriously into account. This is necessary if we are to be attuned to God's creative, revealing, and redemptive presence to all people, and free to be receptive to the insights of all people rather than clinging anxiously to our own traditional ways of thinking and speaking.

One reason why the difference between Christians and non-Christians has so often been exaggerated in the past is that in its missionary life and endeavors the church always wanted to be "on the safe side." With characteristic caution, the church never took unnecessary risks, especially in matters of grace and salvation—where the stakes are indeed high. It would pray as though everything depended on God and, without any fear of contradicting itself, would immediately set out to convert and baptize as though everything depended on itself. Indeed the church has always professed the existence and workings of divine grace outside the visible boundaries of its own structures. In a sense it has always been mindful of the words of St. Augustine: "Many whom God has, the church does not have; and many whom the church has, God does not have." Yet this sincere conviction did not always determine or shape its basic missionary approach and policy. By and large, it was to remain more of a notional belief than a working missionary principle. For all its sympathetic understanding, the church always found difficulty in coming to grips with divine grace in those who did not profess explicit faith in God or Christ.

The church has also consistently professed the universal brotherhood of all people under the fatherhood of God, but here again this idea was never the direct principle of its missionary undertaking. Brotherhood was regarded mainly as a purely "natural" reality, having little or no connection with the redeeming grace of Christ or the immediate life of the church. Consequently, the parallelism and convergence between what Christ was actually doing in the world and what the church was doing in the world was scarcely taken into account. The church did teach that all people are related to God in several ways: as creatures to Creator; as objects of God's love in his care for his human children; as agents for God's will, however brokenly, imperfectly, and sinfully we may respond to that will. But in all these instances the ties were generally envisaged quite independently of the person of Jesus Christ, and hence were not deemed especially Christian in nature. On the whole, the possibility that even a quite secular person might have some genuine experience of divine grace was never a major missionary concern of the church.

Broken Solidarity

Another factor exaggerating the difference between Christians and non-Christians to the point of polarization was the watershed doctrine of original sin. Traditionally, this sinful state was explained by some catastrophic act of choice by our progenitor Adam. In every newborn child, original sin was said to preclude automatically any real grace-full tie with Christ. Only baptism could establish such a bond. Now whatever else may be said about original sin, it cannot simply be described as an absolute "not-yet-in-Christ" situation, a condition of utter Christlessness. As we have seen, no such state really exists or is possible. All people are united to Christ at the deepest level of personal existence prior to baptism and the possibility of their free decision for or against Christ.

It is beyond the scope of our present investigations to examine contemporary approaches to original sin, but since these do have significant bearing on our subject we must consider some aspects of this important question. The first major consideration is that sinfulness does not simply belong to separate individuals; it is characteristic of the human race as a whole. The ongoing power of evil and the pervasiveness of sin in human beings and in human institutions is a reality we read about in Scripture and in our daily newspapers as well. The concept of "original sin" above all embraces the total view of humankind and emphasizes the rupture in human solidarity. Were it not for sin, the unity of the human race would reveal itself both in human consciousness and in the existence of a truly united world family. This idea is brought out strongly in Genesis, where sin is pre-eminently seen as a progressive disruption and division of the human community: between man and woman (3:15), within the human family (4:1–16), in the tribal community of the desert (4:24), and ultimately in the community of nations (11:1–9). The climax of this breakdown in human solidarity is powerfully represented in the story of the Tower of Babel with the ensuing language barrier, the most telling and direct symbol possible. Inner discord, envy, and spitefulness which set people at cross purposes with one another lead to civil discord and the scattering of nations. It was against the background of such general division and strife that salvation from God was later interpreted (Isa. 43:5–6). Christ came to restore the broken unity of humankind driven apart by sin. In him, God was not content to win and possess people separately as so many scattered and dispersed individuals, nor did he limit himself to the sanctification of humanity, unit by unit, individual by individual. Rather he assumed humankind's wounded existence as community in order to recast its broken unity.

The point we wish to stress here is that sin is never *only* a private sin that calls for private confession. By this I do not in the least mean that since we are the product of our sinful environment there is a collective guilt that cancels out personal responsibility. Yet we are linked with others in all our acts, the good as well as the evil. In the domain of sin, the fine distinction between "mine" and "yours" breaks down and is irreducibly subsumed in the all-possessive category of "ours." This is what the concept of original sin above all is meant to convey. We are members of one another both in our evil-doing and in our right-doing. What we do or fail to do has enormous consequences for those around us and for those who come after us.

Léon Bloy vividly describes this chain reaction of sin when he says: "If someone gives a poor man a penny grudgingly, that penny pierces the poor man's hand, falls, pierces the earth, bores holes in suns, crosses the firmament and jeopardizes the universe. If he begets an impure act, he perhaps darkens thousands of hearts whom he does not know, who are mysteriously linked to him." Hence, the solidarity of the human race, however injured or broken, has a great deal to do with the

situation in which we find ourselves. A direct up-
shot of this is that the curse of an evil action goes on,
forever producing evil consequences. The concept
of original sin would thus remind us that the roots
of evil are still very much alive within the human
community and that we stand by inner necessity
under the contagious power of sin.

Abounding Grace

Although sin spins its net around us in the most
varied manner and through innumerable means,
the inherited gracefullness of Christ's redemptive
and continuing Incarnation counteracts this sinful
sway. It is inconceivable that the Incarnation of the
Son of God made less of an impact on humanity
than the Fall of Adam. Too often in the past we have
made original sin universal and have particularized
redemption, as though Adam had carved his ini-
tials deeper on the flesh of humanity than had
Christ. As we have already pointed out, human
solidarity as such is impartial and plays no favor-
ites. All things being equal, it lends itself just as
readily and without contradiction to negative influ-
ences as to positive ones. However, we know
through divine revelation that all things are *not*
equal. Our solidarity with Christ through grace is
more universal, more decisive, and more efficacious than is our solidarity with Adam through sin.
The beneficial influence of the former far exceeds
the detrimental power of the latter. It has always

been the teaching conviction of the church that grace is stronger than sin and that whatever harm had been done to humankind by the Old Adam was superabundantly restituted by the New Adam. This eminent restoration means, if anything, that the attractive force of Christ is more decisive than the sinful weight of Adam. Or to put it in another way, human weakness—even human wickedness —is invariably weaker than the triumphant power of God's grace. In the present economy of salvation, we are more stringently bound and prepossessed by Christ than by Adam.

This does not mean that our solidarity with Adam is automatically destroyed or broken. Not even God could do that without at the same time destroying our very nature. Human solidarity not only remains, but it remains ambivalent and thus supports sharply contrasting values. It simultaneously places us in solidarity with sinners as well as with the more righteous, with the Old Adam and with the New. Seen in this context of the Adam-Christ parallel, original sin and original grace are not mutually exclusive. Indeed, as St. Augustine put it: "Every man is Adam and every man is Christ." Hence human destiny must be inexorably worked out within this ambivalent solidarity. From our very first breath we are all in a state of original sin and original grace.

In order to overcome this "impossible" situation, we are obliged to make a fundamental option, one way or the other, and remain uncompromisingly faithful to that option. For there can be no real option unless it is ratified, consummated, and bodied forth in the whole series of daily acts that form the basic fabric of our lives. It must be an orientation that we freely choose and would give to our entire lives. However, we are unable to do this on our own; we are like weathervanes exposed to every crosswind and current. The concept of original sin defines this general state of dissipation. Since we are unable to "live up" to our original union with Christ, we are unavoidably condemned to make sinful compromise. We are born prodigals who are not able, without further assistance from God, to personally orientate our whole lives toward Christ.

Despite the fact that we are all united to Christ from the very beginning through an original grace, we can nevertheless reject and disengage ourselves from Christ. Yet this rejection, like that of Adam, always takes place *within* grace. It is never simply the refusal of an external invitation or offer of grace; it is always the rejection of grace already founded in us, a radical "I will live with you no more." Hence every sinner is a prodigal in the strictest sense of the word, and every sin, original or otherwise, is invariably a squandering of God's loving presence in us.

Today there is a growing Christian awareness of the anonymous presence and workings of grace in the lives of all people, and with this heightened awareness the difference between Christians and non-Christians, between believers and non-believers, is no longer being regarded in absolute terms. This conviction is supported by a better understanding of the basic unity of the whole process of salvation. Scripture presents salvation, of humankind and of every individual, as something in the process of realization. The total reality of salvation has its beginning in our radical solidarity with Christ, its progressive unfolding in a living, personal fellowship and friendship with Christ, and its consummation in glory. When we come into existence, we are germinally baptized in Christ, redeemed people to whom Christ is personally present. Even though we ourselves are not aware of this, everything about this truly original grace points to a life of faith that is still to come, a conversion, the decision to follow Christ, and the basic will to fulfill the conditions laid down by Christ for those who would be his true friends. Yet even this new life of intimate friendship with Christ must grow and mature, advance and increase. While still in this world we must await yet another event that will confirm us in the vision of God's glory.

These temporal aspects of the process of salvation are all interconnected and very often overlap one another in our actual experience of them. It is impossible to separate them, for in reality they complement, penetrate, and mutually illuminate one another far beyond our knowing. When this fundamental unity of salvation as a process is perceived clearly, there is less danger of exaggerating the difference between Christians and non-Christians. As members of the saved race, non-Christians or non-believers are not simply people; they are redeemed people, germinally baptized in Christ and personally in touch with divine grace. The "fact-of-being-redeemed" cannot be understood, as some theologians still contend today, on the analogy of what is meant by saying about a drowning man that he is safe or saved as soon as a rescue boat comes near to him. Christ is not only at hand to rescue us, nor is his saving hand merely extended and offered. Christ has in fact laid hands on us, seized and taken hold of us at the deepest level of personal existence. Were they fully conscious of this, redeemed non-Christians could repeat St. Paul's words with an amazing amount of truth: "Christ has laid hold of men" (Phil. 3:12). This personal grasp that Christ has on all people at the seemingly uncanny, bottomless depth of our being is nothing less than a sanctifying hold. This is more than an offer of grace and a call to salvation. It is a state of grace in which we originally find ourselves, a state that personally constitutes for us an abiding and transforming contact with Christ. The intrinsic reality of redemption is that the Son of God has united himself with all people. This personal union with Christ, which is the essential truth of all grace, admits various degrees, as does the human personal order into which Christ entered.

Christian tradition has always clearly maintained that personal union with Christ can grow deeper, more transforming, more freely implanted in us and that growth in grace is possible. This growth rises in ascending stages from baptism to explicit, credal confession of faith, to recognition of the authority of the visible church, full participation in its sacramental life, and ultimately to the attainment of eternal blessedness. The Christian life of grace bears the authentic stamp of growth firmly imprinted on it. Accordingly, divine grace is said to help the remiss to become good, the good to become better, the better to become even more generous, the generous to become saints. To sanctity, it suggests new ways of manifesting itself; it sharpens love to the point of exquisite inventiveness and forever elicits new enthusiasm for Christian heroism. No one would deny that this is a faithful description of Christians' inspired understanding of their call to perfection. What we are suggesting here is that just as there are ascending stages of grace rising from baptism, so there are descending stages going down from the explicitness of faith and baptism into the deeper reaches of our radical solidarity with Christ which can and must be called real grace.

To speak of grace at all is to speak of the way in which God and human beings are personally present to one another in Christ. Like Christians, non-Christians stand in a positive relation to Christ and have been touched by the reality of Christ's redemption. To this extent, the reality of grace is not foreign to them. Whether they realize it or not, there exists a basic affinity between their solidarity with Christ and that of the baptized Christian. The difference between the two is no less significant for being relative, but it does mean that what they have in common outweighs anything that may divide them.

Since grace does admit various degrees—even infinite degrees—it can therefore never be adequately formulated or "contained" in neat theological categories. Grace spills over and abounds on all sides of our every attempt to define it. And this, first, because all formulations are necessarily more restrictive than comprehensive and, second, because God's capacity for self-communication in and through Christ knows no limits—indeed delights in going beyond all limits. This "overspill" of divine grace has always bedeviled theologians and ultimately explains why they can speak of universal grace only in the most probing and tentative manner. Yet it is quite clear that the abounding, universal nature of God's grace is an essential truth of grace.

Nowhere is this abounding nature of divine grace more apparent than in the biblical theme of Election. When God chooses a person, a people, a special history of salvation, his love is in no way exclusively restricted to his chosen ones. On the contrary, such particular elections are designed to offer his divine mercy and love many channels through which it can flow swiftly to all people, wherever they may be. Election always means grace for others than the elect, in ways that far exceed any-

thing that we could dream of or expect. To interpret
God's gift of grace to his Christian people as excluding the others is therefore just as reproachable as
Israel's narrow understanding of its own election.
As Scripture repeatedly illustrates, God is forever
breaking through the limits which he himself has
set up. The empty grave of Christ, the one who was
himself emptied, is perhaps the most telling sign of
the way God deals with us. Any theology of grace,
therefore, which would try to contain within strict
national boundaries "him whom the whole world
cannot contain" will sooner or later find itself as
empty as a tomb. If we endeavor to seal off the
Christian state of grace from that of the non-Christians, we are quite likely to discover, to our conster-
nation, that the risen Lord is forever passing
through closed doors.

The grace-full affinity that exists between non-
Christians and Christians can also be approached
from the point of view of the specifically Christian
brotherhood that unites all people in a truly universal bond. When we are born into the world we are
true brothers or sisters of Jesus, the Son of God.
Kinship in Jesus Christ is written both as a fact and
as a necessity in human nature. Through the Incarnation, the Son of God made man is inserted into
the intricate tapestry of the human personal order.
He thereby enters into relation with all people and
so unifies and centralizes in himself all created relationships. Thus all human beings, wherever they
may be born, are by definition not only *possible*

brothers or sisters of Christ, but are in fact *real* brothers or sisters of him. They are literally of one blood with Christ. Although they are not everything that God would have them be, they are nevertheless pre-possessed by this Christic kinship, which must somehow dawn upon their consciousness and become a deeper, more intimate, form of belonging to Christ.

Since God became human, grace has entered into the inmost, secret core of humanity and Christian kinship is inscribed on the heart of all people born into the world. It is a kind of grace in existence itself. Without always realizing it, all people are searching amid the myriad enigmas of human existence for the true face of their Brother who is already there as a Stranger. They long for Christ just as surely as they long for the discovery of their own identity and fulfillment. There is no sure guarantee that all people will succeed in discovering Christ as *their own* brother, nor indeed that they will not disown Christ once they find him. Yet even though they do not reach their goal, even if they fall by the wayside, they will nevertheless have experienced something of the Christian joy of having run, strained, and sweated as much as they could, in search of the face of their Lord and Savior.

The best Christian tradition has always recognized in human nature something that is naturally Christian and has consistently maintained that even the most specifically human aspirations, joys, hopes, and fulfillment are somehow related to

Christ. Even at the risk of appearing somewhat arrogant and haughty in the eyes of the world, the church has taught that any goodness and sanctity found to exist "outside" its own visible frontiers mysteriously belongs to itself because it belongs to Christ. It is important that Christians be reminded of this. Today more than ever, they ought to be prepared to recognize in everyone the face of Christ and claim for their Lord every good deed, every noble thought, every brave act, every creation of beauty, every life of humble service and every genuine religious aspiration, no matter where or under what conditions these may appear. Wherever people strive after truth and goodness in honesty of heart, whenever they sacrifice and wear themselves out in the service of their neighbors, particularly the poor, the afflicted, and the downtrodden, Christ is personally present and at work. In all such expressions of our deepest soul, the hidden grace of God is more operative than we are usually willing to suppose or admit. This means that when we approach non-Christians, it is not just to bring Christ to them, but to bring Christ out of them. Such a claim is valid on the grounds that universal grace is not a myth but a reality, and that every person is in reality the true brother or sister of Christ.

The Sign of the Cross

This fraternal bond between Christians and non-

Christians, between believers and non-believers, is particularly called into account in moments of personal crisis and decision. Whenever unbelievers are confronted with human suffering, which they must either accept in sacrifice or reject in revolt; whenever they must choose between vengeance and pardon at the sudden realization that a bitter hatred for someone has entered into their hearts; whenever they are forced to decide, after suddenly falling in love with another person's spouse, whether they will break up a legitimate marriage or renounce their new happiness; whenever they are sorely pressed by circumstances to choose between justice and a dishonest deal that could make them rich—in all such crucial instances of agonizing decision, these people are never alone. From all appearances, they may seem alone and left to their own inner resources. They may not have anyone in whom they can or dare confide, on whom they can lean, or with whom they can decide. Nobody! And yet, the grace of God is with them. The presence of Christ and all the believing Christians are with them. At the very moment they must work out, by themselves, the drama of their response, unbelievers are surrounded, supported, and carried forth by the hidden and innumerable presence of their Christian brothers and sisters. They are together through prayers and offering, hope and silent sacrifices. This action that is taken by unknown brothers and sisters on behalf of their unknown kin is inspired by Christ, who knows them all personally and is a brother to all. It is the exercise of the wider "communion of saints." On account of their common kinship in Christ, Christians and non-Christians form only one family among themselves and all have some share in the grace of Christ.

There is yet another aspect to this common kinship in Christ that cannot be too strongly emphasized—all live under the sign of the Cross. If the bond of Christian kinship is particularly activated in those moments when a person is called to make a crucial and far-reaching decision in life, it comes powerfully into play in moments of great suffering. Here we see that all people are united together in Christ, the Man of Sorrows. This participation in the mystery of the Cross spotlights still better the reality of Christian kinship.

All people live in the same world torn by human suffering, are embedded in it, and are bound by its laws and dependent on its conditions. Yet in the mystery of Christ's redemption, all human suffering now refers, and is somehow linked, to the Cross that saves the world. All people who suffer are united to Christ even if, explicitly, they know nothing of Christ—but only the Cross. In this crucifying communion, all people bear something of Christ's suffering in their own persons, know something of Christ's wounds on their bodies, are crucified with Christ, and thus help to fill up those things that are wanting in the sufferings of Christ. All this is possible because Christ became a real brother to all people and thus *our* cross becomes *his* Cross. When the

Cross enters our lives, it invariably comes as a great
trial and an agonizing ordeal. Like a two-edged
sword, it can make us cry out in despair and revolt,
or else wrench from us a heart-rending plea for
help. It inflicts either the pain of death or the pain of
resurrection. The Cross is often the only thing in life
that can unlock an otherwise closed, self-centered
existence. It can tear us from ourselves and awaken
in our soul even the most deeply repressed and
suffocated longing for God. Its crucifying power
can crack open the heart of even the most seasoned,
die-hard sinners, and it does this by suddenly calling into question everything in their lives and
drawing out of them, perhaps for the first time, a
plea for mercy and forgiveness. Then, and sometimes only then, through this small fissure of vulnerability, can the hidden grace of God surface and
bring them into a more intimate union with Christ.
The Cross is thus a powerful sign of grace since it
can drive even the most pitiful person into the arms
of God, as it did the good thief who was crucified
with Jesus.

There is another kind of suffering that cannot be
ignored today since it constitutes the basic fabric of
so many lives and stretches out over long periods of
time in people's lives—indeed, for millions of people, throughout their whole lives. This suffering
comes as extreme poverty with its long retinue of
human misery. What makes this heritage of poverty so intolerably great and pernicious is that it
exerts its full power to destroy by poisoning the

very springs of life and crushes the inmost fibers of personal existence. It is the kind of suffering that reduces human beings, brothers and sisters in Christ, to a subhuman level. Not only does it kill, but it cripples and leads to all sorts of physical, psychological, and moral deformity. It spawns lives without prospects, without hope; lives foundering in fatalism and degraded by a begging mentality. This long, drawn-out disintegration of human life cries up to heaven against us as long as we do nothing to overcome it.

God looks upon the poor differently than we do. God sees them through his Christ, who one day mysteriously identified himself with them and became a brother to all. He even made of the second commandment, "You will love your neighbor as yourself," the sign and means of fulfilling the first. And at the end of our lives, he will judge us all according to the criterion of love. This means that when even unbelievers are confronted with an urgent plea for help, often not even articulated in words, whenever they meet another in distress and are the only ones to help, they stand before the greatest commandment of Christ—indeed before Christ in person. If they say, "Yes," and make of themselves neighbors to the other—that is to those whose need constitutes a claim on their love—it will be a sign that the grace of Christ is silently at work in them. This is brought out very clearly in the parable of the Good Samaritan. In this story, the example of a semi-pagan foreigner, a Samaritan, is set before us to illustrate the true Christian attitude toward others. Jesus deliberately shocks us by forcing us, as he did the devout Jewish lawyer, to consider the possibility that even a heretic and an idolater might know more about the love of God than we Christians.

It is in fact quite remarkable that in the parable of the Last Judgment (Matt. 25), those who had given food to the hungry, or drink to the thirsty, or harbored the stranger, clothed the naked, visited the sick, or consoled the prisoner, did not realize at the time of their action that they had in fact been standing before Christ. Nor did those who were delinquent in these acts of mercy. Both groups were ignorant of Christ. In view of this general state of ignorance, one must therefore take their question seriously: "Master, when did we see you hungry or thirsty, a stranger or naked, sick or in prison?" The answer that our Lord gave was not: "When you *realized* or *thought* that it was me," but rather: "Inasmuch as you *did* this to one of these least brethren of mine, you did it to me."

Non-Christians will be judged in this same way, not on their clear understanding or their explicit knowledge, but on their acts of love and everything love implies. Since the most obscure movement toward another is a sign that Christ's spirit is already present, and since an act of love can substitute for the lack of explicit faith and baptism, such people are not so very different from their Christian brothers and sisters. The grace that prompts them to the selfless service of the poor in everyday life is not essentially different from that which inspires Christians to do the same. While admitting a degree of difference, the Christ-like affinity that exists between Christian and non-Christian unites them more closely than anything that may otherwise separate them.

Christians today must therefore be reminded that under no pretext must they create an essential division of superiority and subordination between themselves and non-Christians. Universal kinship in Christ precludes any such division, for it is the exercise of an existential unity, the result of being personally related to Christ, the experience of a "we" in its deepest, most primitive, Christian form. This solidarity in grace between Christians and non-Christians takes priority over all other differences that may occur in the order of grace.

5

Church and World

Through twenty centuries of history the church and the world have experienced a wide variety of relationships, ranging from fierce rivalry and hatred to peaceful coexistence, from power struggle to uncaring cynicism, "from anathema to dialogue." Under persecution or the threat of persecution the church withdrew as far as it could from the world, seeking to conceal itself from people who were constantly doing their best to trap it, asking hostile questions, twisting the meaning of its words, and denouncing it to the civil authorities. At other times, when relationships were better, hostility and suspicion gave way to feelings of mutual regard. There were even times when the church and the world were closely united in what seemed to be a happy *ménage à deux*. They would have their quarrels of course, but on the whole there existed between the two a deeply felt need for each other and a profound interdependence.

The world would come to learn, however, that

the church does not make the best of marriage partners and is not always immune to certain individualized forms of the pathology of love. Conscious of itself as a mother figure, it could at times become extremely possessive and domineering—seeking to bring the whole world into the embrace of Christendom, or clasping Christians so tightly to its maternal bosom that they could not breathe. In its more helpless moments, the church would seek the world's protection, love, and admiration. These times of great uncertainty were usually characterized by the experience of an identity crisis, a loss on the church's part of its I-ness and sense of mission.

Occasionally alienated from its own powers, the church would throw itself into the arms of the world with a passion akin to that of a certain type of idolatrous love, as though the world was the bearer of all knowledge, all light, all wisdom. At the opposite extreme, it could behave like a nagging marriage partner, developing an almost obsessive concern with the defects and "wrongs" of the world as though it could see nothing else. And it often seemed as if this preoccupation kept the church too busy to consider its own shortcomings and reform itself. This attitude often gave rise to the irritating tendency to blame the world for its own spiritual problems. Hence any decline in religious fervor or priestly vocations was usually attributed in the first instance to the permissiveness of society, the secularization of thought, or the materialistic atmosphere of the world.

Brothers in Partnership

Our purpose here is not to describe all the difficulties that can and do arise between the church and the world, but to indicate the inadequacy of viewing the church-world relationships through the model of marriage partners. There are certainly many different models that could be used to describe these relationships. An early father of the church described them this way: "The world without the church is like a body without a soul, but the church without the world is like a soul without a body." The analogy is somewhat weakened if we consider the rather low esteem in which the human body was held when these words were written and the correspondingly high value placed on the human soul. Nevertheless, the idea of complementarity is no less stressed.

Of all possible models, we would strongly suggest that the model of brothers *in partnership* is the most satisfactory, partly because it is one that speaks loud and clear to our modern times, and especially because it takes universal grace seriously into account.

The Second Vatican Council certainly endorsed this model of fraternal partnership when it set out to describe what ought to be the relationship between the church and the world. The Council viewed the church and the world as two inseparable companions going down the road of history together, collaborating closely, each giving the oth-

er something without which neither could really go
it alone. In his opening speech at the second session
of the Council, Pope Paul VI beautifully described
this new outlook that would animate the most tradi-
tion-encrusted of churches: "The world should
know that the church constantly looks at her, sincerely admires her, and sincerely intends not to
dominate but to serve, not to despise her but to
increase her dignity, not to condemn her, but to
bring her comfort and salvation."

Healthy relationships between the church and
the world are possible only if the two partners
communicate the way brothers do, each from the
center of his own existence. The mutual attachment
of brothers necessarily gives rise to what we may
call "confidences"—that is, a trustful looking for
help from each other in concerns and experiences
that belong already to the future. In their lives,
brothers are in the deepest sense permanently connected. Thus, whether there is harmony or conflict,
joy or sadness in the relationship becomes secondary to the more fundamental fact that both experience themselves as brothers, that they are one with
each other by being one with themselves.

Before investigating the reality of this fraternal
partnership more closely, a preliminary remark is
called for. We must think of the church here as a
community of persons, or better still a corporate
person; and so, in the same way that individuals
need encounter with other persons in order to be-

come their true selves, the church as a moral person comes into its own only by being confronted with its historical partner, the world. What is important in this encounter is not a total understanding between the church and the world but a working relationship and mutual appreciation. Each will remain in some manner a mystery to the other. The proper integration of the church-world relationships requires neither total comprehension nor mutual exclusion; it consists rather in an interplay of tensions that are both functional and creative.

The *first* thing that must be said of brothers in partnership is that while they collaborate very closely they nevertheless retain their inherent differences. This is particularly true of the church and the world. There can be no question of the one being mistaken for the other; both remain what they are, quite distinct, and autonomous in their own right and in their respective sphere of duty. In fact it is only because they have a life and vocation of their own that it is possible to speak of dialogue and fraternal partnership between the two. When we consider that salvation takes place outside the visible church for the greater part of humankind and that vocation to the church in the sense of membership is not yet offered by God to everyone, we begin to appreciate more fully the grace-full dimension of this partnership. We also begin to realize that salvation can no longer be regarded as the exclusive vocation or reserve of either partner.

Both the church and the world are instrumental in the work of salvation and both are embodiments of God's grace.

For the church, this means that a contempt for the world which leaves little or no room for positive values in the temporal order borders on blasphemy. It also means that Christians are not to use created things only as a ladder in their ascent to God, or the world only as an occasion or background of their charitable deeds and spiritual purification. The inability or unwillingness to cherish and respect the inherent positive value of terrestrial realities has a predictable effect, particularly when it comes to charity and almsgiving. Christians give, not because the recipient "deserves" anything, but for other reasons of their own. Indeed, the gesture of the giver is not really addressed to the recipient at all. The deed is, as it is often said, done for God. The receiver is thus a mere occasion and exists for the sake of the giver, that is, for the latter's righteous stance before God. The inherent dignity of the person who receives is effectively obliterated. This example typifies much of the church's past approach to the world. Today, however, the church is being converted to the intrinsic value of the world in its texture of earthly realities. In his own prophetic way, Teilhard de Chardin envisaged just such a conversion when he said: "In my opinion, the world will not be converted to the heavenly promises of Christianity unless Christianity has previously been converted to the promises of the earth."

There is a second aspect of this partnership that God has set up between the church and the world: Both work unto the same end, both are seeking basically the same thing, namely the perfection and success of people, and with people of the world. Whether in the church or in the world, God's saving activity steers toward one and the same end of history, that is, the perfect community and unity of all people through Christ in God, to the kingdom of God in its fulfillment. There is but *one* history, and all history is *sacred*. It is within such a unified vision of history that the church and the world are seen to exist and function as historical partners. They do not stand over against one another, nor do they rival or compete with one another; rather, both serve one another and in so doing are at the disposal of God's ultimate aim. It is inconceivable that God's action in the church and his action in the world should be working for two different historical aims.

This means in practice that the process of biological evolution, the decisions and actions of people in history, and the life and worship of the church are integrally related. Through all these it is the same God who works to complete his creation, impelling all from within toward his purposes. To participate with confidence in the technological transformation of creation, in the processes of society and liberation, and in the mission of the church are equally and inseparably aspects of our "total" vocation. Thus, nothing genuinely human can fail to raise an echo in the hearts of Christians, nor can anything genuinely Christian fail to stir the hearts of secular humanists.

A third characteristic of true brothers is that their natural affinity and "being used to each other" does not exclude every kind of opposition. Contrast is essential in brotherhood. The marvel is how it can tolerate such wide differences and reconcile them in a single bond of fraternal unity. Brotherhood between the church and the world is no exception; it is often uneasy and knows moments of considerable tension and conflict. Indeed, the church has often found itself in conflict with the world—conflict with the scientific world (Galileo); conflict with the economic world (usury); conflict with a world "coming of age" (secularization); conflict with a world becoming overpopulated (contraception). This list could be continued, but more important than an inventory of conflicts is the basic reason why there will always be a certain amount of antagonism and periods of great tension between these two brothers.

Although the Christian message is in harmony with the most secret desires of the human heart, it is also a challenge to, and not infrequently a judgment upon, the world. By becoming more and more identified in faith with its Lord, who was foolishness for the wise, a stumbling-block for the pious, and a trouble maker for the powerful, the church will invariably find itself at times in bitter opposition to the world. Only when it has the courage to be and act differently from the world can it really mean something to the world. The question therefore is not whether the church always sees eye-to-eye with the world and agrees with it on every score, but how well the church finds both its identity and its relevance in the cross of Christ. The Crucified One shows that God's mercy must reveal itself in the world, so that we may become fully conscious of his guilt and his redemption.

The church should always try to take a positive attitude toward the world's difficulties. It must develop a deep understanding if it is to penetrate to the world's real concern, which is so often hidden under the surface of things. And it must use this sympathetic insight whenever it has to correct erroneous ideas and attitudes in the world. At times, this obligation for fraternal correction and exhortation must give way to a more drastic stimulus of change and reform, namely the obligation of outspoken prophecy. Many people think of a prophet as someone who predicts the future. When it comes to futurology, the world is usually more reliable and its predictions more accurate. Here the term "prophet" is used in a much wider sense to denote one who does not hesitate to question certain apparently established elements in his environment, or indeed an entire social system or outlook. In the Old Testament, the prophets were above all people of their times, people who were deeply concerned about the problems of society and whose prophetic utterances were aimed at arousing the sluggish conscience of their generation. In fulfilling this task, they did not mince their words or take time for the finer shades of meaning and niceties of language; theirs was a passionate language with all the unexpected bluntness and shrillness of a cry from the heart. It was in this same prophetic tradition that Jesus made the cry of the oppressed his own cry when he proclaimed "happy the poor" and "woe to the rich."

The cutting edge of the prophets' words serve as a constant reminder to the church that it must not regard its faith as an evasion, but as a real commitment; it must practice what it preaches, and only to that extent will its prophetic utterances ring true. Authenticity is the only sure criterion for distinguishing real prophets from false prophets and the church too must pass this test. If there is any truth in the serious charge that "religion is the opium of the people," it can only be so when the church neglects its prophetic role and fails to denounce the injustices in the world, from whatever system they arise; when it is not critical enough of the established order and not sufficiently sensitive in facing its inhuman aspects. The church knows only too well that before it can pass judgment on its partner, the world, it stands itself under judgment. When its prophetic voice falls silent, it is sometimes because the words of Christ suddenly ring in its own ears:

"How dare you say to your brother, 'Let me take the splinter out of your eye,' when all the time there is a plank in your own? Hypocrite! Take the plank out of your own eye first, and then you will see clearly enough to take the splinter out of your brother's eye" (Matt. 7:3–5).

The relationship between the church and the world is generally described in terms of the church *in* the world. By this of course is meant that the church—like leaven in dough or light in darkness—is immersed in the world, exists in history, and has a mission to the world. By this is also meant a small church in a large world, a minority community in the service of the majority. But, looking at the matter the other way around, there is a real sense in which the world can be said to be *in* the church and to be the "salt" and "light" of the church. It is our intention here to develop this neglected aspect of the church-world partnership and to spell out in greater detail the mission of the world in the church.

While it is certain that the world cannot realistically hope to fulfill its function in saving history without the church, it must also be recognized that the church cannot succeed in its own vocation without the aid and service of the historical partner given it by God. The church is in the world and the world in is the church. What we are talking about here is more than simply a matter of cross-fertilization and certainly much more than a well-oiled relationship of team spirit. Rather it is a question of real compenetration between the church and the world—a term that Vatican II did not consider too strong to describe the church-world correlation (*Gaudium et Spes,* nos. 40, 3).

We are thus brought to our central consideration of how the world can legitimately be said to function *in* the church. It is important first of all to distinguish, on the one hand, the help which the church receives from the world occasionally and indirectly, and on the other hand, the vital functions that the world fulfills for and in the church. While these two aspects can and often do overlap in practice, they are not the same. An example will help to illustrate the difference. Mathematics and physics are two sciences that compenetrate each other. This does not mean that mathematics simply offers considerable help to its sister science when and if desired; rather, it means that mathematics exercises, within physics itself, a pivotal function. Similarly, the world performs a crucial and multi-faceted role in the church.

Not only does the church receive ancillary aid from the world, such as the expertise of those who live in the world, the definite advantages of modern communications, the findings of sociologists and other scientists; but over and above these real benefits there are some specific areas in which the world constantly functions in the service of the church. These functions are neither optional nor sporadic; rather they are vital to the very life of the church and, consequently, are exercised by the world in an ongoing, around-the-clock fashion. Without such abiding and crucial support, the church would not be the reality it is. Our investigation of some of the more important functions of the world *in* the church will enable us to appreciate more fully the fraternal partnership that exists between the two and the further implications of universal grace.

Catholic Function

The world is *in* the church, first of all, because it constitutes an essential part of the church's catholicity. As Yves Congar has often stated, the catholicity of the church—that intrinsic, universal capacity for unity—is derived from a dual source: the risen Lord who brings all things more perfectly together in himself unto God, but also the world and the virtually infinite resources of human nature. It is this second source that we would like to emphasize here.

The world enables the church to realize its catholicity in that it enables the church to grow organically through the assimilation of all the marvelous wealth and variety of human values, persons, races, classes, or cultures. Without these, the church would not in fact be universal. With these, the world offers the church the *real possibility* of embracing, enhancing, and perfecting the whole variety of gifts in the world and the whole diversity of humankind redeemed by Christ. In this way, the church is summoned to be present to all human situations at each hour of history and is called by the world to become all things to all people in the name of the Lord. In short, the world constantly opens out new perspectives and real possibilities for the church, without which it could not be truly catholic.

We must not understand this to mean that the world is simply the "stuff" out of which the church realizes its catholicity, as it might be said, for example, of a builder who uses wood to construct his house. Rather, the real possibilities that the world opens out to the church are to be understood in a dynamic sense. As the realm of possible being, the world is not passive and indifferent; objectively real possibilities exist in it and these strongly suggest, of themselves, newness of life and meaning for the church. In effect, this means that the church continually receives from the world the possibility of actualizing its message. It also means that the world is forever revealing in dream and anticipation that which could or might be, indeed that which ought to be. Thus the world is a promise to the church, a hope of a fulfillment that will someday find "all things in Christ " (Eph. 1:10).

It is not too difficult to understand why the church is generally so conservative in the face of the world and why it is so slow in seizing the untold possibilities to which the world continually calls it. In the infinite possibilities of its future, the world will always be something of a mysterious partner, that is, unknown or inadequately known. The unknown can be appealing and attractive, but it can also be frightening, indeed terrifying at times.

Since the world is the realm of all possible being, it invariably functions in the church in the most ambivalent fashion. At times the world will appear to the church as wonderful (in the sense of bringing possible wonders which cause amazement), awful (in the sense of inspiring awe), terrible (in the sense of awakening terror), overwhelming (in the sense of being beyond control and demanding a certain passive acquiescence). At other times, the world will appear as gracious, enabling, and fulfilling. It will always continue to threaten or invite the church, to attract or distract, to summon or demand. Through this liberating tension, out of which future possibilities arise, the church is given courage to acknowledge what is lacking in its catholicity and to make its life and action more all-embracing.

The result of this catholic partnership between the church and the world is always something *new*. If humankind is to mature toward its final coronation in the all-embracing Christ, this can only be achieved if the church and the world make history together by creating the future. What is required is imagination, creativity, and decision. In its catholic function, the world makes the church realize ever anew and ever differently that the possible future of both partners is at once a human affair and a divine task. Thus the world gives the church ever more courage and decision in undertaking the seemingly impossible and certainly risky tasks that the future imposes. It assures the church of its active resources and dynamic collaboration, and thus guarantees its catholicity.

Theological Function

A second important function that the world exercises in the church is what we call its theological function: The world leads the church to a more reflective and clearer grasp of its own nature and message. The truth of the church must always be more deeply penetrated, better understood, and set forth to greater advantage. In this important respect, the world mirrors the church in concrete historical events and thus brings the church to a sharper awareness of the presence of God's word in history as well as to a better understanding of itself and its mission. That, after all, is the law of all living things.

Modern psychology has clearly shown that we perceive who we are by seeing ourselves reflected in the reactions of others. Our personality is shaped by the reactions of people we encounter, in the very profound sense that it is from their reactions that we learn to appreciate and better understand what is good in us. Thus our hidden talents, aspirations, and splendid dreams can become real only when we are able to mirror them in someone else. The same laws obtain in the relationships between the church and the world. The church comes to a better understanding of itself and its faith when it mirrors itself in the world and in the contemporary experience of all people. In a very real sense, the world is the looking-glass self of the church. The reflection in this mirror is of great importance since the "signs of the times" are a voice, for the church, either of the presence of God or of the absence of God.

By listening to the world of people and discerning God's voice in it, the church is able to refocus the gospel for its own age. Otherwise it would continue simply to advance answers to questions the world is no longer asking. Hence one of the main functions of the modern world is to raise questions the church has never seriously thought of. By raising such "impertinent" questions the world engages the attention of the church, which would not otherwise be addressed, and thus initiates a conversation. The world thus creates a new self-consciousness in the church and leads the church into a new way of experiencing itself and a new way of relating the Good News of the gospel to its environment.

It is this process, evoked by the ongoing theological function of the world in the church, which produces a reformulation and development of doctrine. Historically, the reflex knowledge and conceptual grasp which the church gradually gained of its own faith was brought about by the reactions of the Jews and pagans to whom the church's message was first directed. However badly damaged the mirror may have been, it was still through this looking-glass self that the church's development of dogma took place. This remains true today. Some of our most profound insights into human nature and the meaning of life come to us through the writings of secular humanists and atheists. When this occurs, the church (a little late and reluctantly at times) accepts these ideas from the non-Christian environment and absorbs them into its theology.

A good recent example of this process may be seen in the outstanding contribution of the Marxist philosopher Ernst Bloch to the theology of hope. His main contribution undoubtedly lies in alerting theologians to the dynamism in their own neglected heritage and in stimulating a preoccupation with the future. One can say without exaggeration that he is chiefly responsible for the genesis of the still immature Christian theologies of hope and revolution—not because he has lent them form, but because he has blessed them with energy, vision, and imagination.

The same could be said of the impact which modern sociology has had in reshaping ecclesiology, that is, the church's understanding of itself. Even when the church appears to be mainly preoccupied with its own life and internal organization, it is never withdrawn from society. Empirical social research has in fact yielded much material that has been taken up by the church, particularly about the actual working of the authority system within the church as well as religious consciousness in a secular world. It is clear that the theoretical concerns of the sociologists do in fact meet the theological concerns of the religiously engaged. The human being that the sociologist studies is the same human being about whom the theologian speaks.

This can be seen in the fact that sociology is no longer considered simply an adjunct of, or preliminary study for, pastoral theology but an integral component of it. Through its theological capacity, the world promotes a sociological awareness on the part of the church and thus prevents it from encapsulating itself in its own tradition and circles. It gives the church ever more perfect eyes, the developing power to see into the mystery of God's people more deeply. Moreover, since the objective unfolding of Christ takes place in history, the world is able to mirror the faith of the church and to make partially but increasingly visible the object of this faith. In this way the world exercises an ongoing theological function in the church, without which the church could not remain perfectly true to itself.

The World as Reminder

We have seen how the world functions in the church as a gift embodying a call, as something potentially enriching for the church and its catholicity. It is a call that summons the church to theological reflection and missionary response. There is another important function that the world exercises in the church, namely, to jog the church's memory.

Basically and first of all, the world obliges the church to "remember" something it already knows through divine revelation, but in practice often tends to forget: the grace-given character of its existence. Here, to remember means much more than merely recalling to the memory. It is more than mental recollection; it must be a concrete remembering—that is, something tangibly experienced as a contemporary reality, an experience that assists the church in its direction and its actions. The world is able to perform such a function in that it is constantly putting the church off-balance, so that it is thrown back, so to speak, upon the Holy Spirit, rather than relying upon its human resources. By its own spirit of total self-reliance the world never allows the church to forget that it exists and is borne on only by the Spirit of God.

The world also serves the church by being a showcase of our sinfulness. Through its press, radio, and live TV coverage the world brings home to everyone in the most vivid possible way human sinfulness and the consequences of sin. In many respects the world acknowledges its sinfulness more readily, and certainly more publicly, than the church does its own. The sheer visibility and stark exposure that the world gives to human alienation confront the church with its own failure and sinfulness. This in turn must invariably bring the church to its knees in humble prayer for pardon before God. Although the church realizes that sinfulness is far more widespread than its own responsibility will carry, it is nonetheless made sorely aware of its real, if limited, complicity. As the realm of human sinfulness, the world has its own way of reminding the church of its own sin and need for pardon.

In this same capacity, the world also serves as a

counter-model to the Christian community and, as such, constantly obliges the church to question itself and re-examine its life and basic position. To make our point, we will indicate some of the more embarrassing questions that the world puts to the church.

Does the church, unlike the *capitalist world*, grow and build itself up through love, as St. Paul said it should? Or does it try to build itself up through the prestige of ecclesiastical authority and a certain moral imperialism? Is the church a community in which the members at the bottom are just as "interesting" and privileged as those at the top, or does powerful bureaucracy even here occasion the alienation of some of its lay people and clergy? Is the church, unlike the highly *industrialized world*, a community in which there is more finality than organization, more conviction than method, more message than medium, more faith and order than law and order? Is the church a community that operates not on the basis of production-consumption, supply-demand, but on the Christian basis of faith, hope, and love? Where quality is not sacrificed for quantity and yet where large numbers do not mean a "lonely crowd," but a living community? Unlike the time-conscious *jet world*, is the church a community in which it is still possible to stop others to ask directions and in which the flow of life does include time lost to strangers who have lost their way? Where time does not mean money and where the future does not come as a sudden shock, but as a long-waited bridegroom? Where we can still bear to be in a room by ourselves, alone with our thoughts and our God? Unlike the *secular world,* where God does not exist or is said not to exist, is the church a people who have experienced, spoken to, and above all wrestled with God? A people who have been conquered by God and through this defeat publish hope in God's victory in the face of the enemies of human life?

These are some of the many questions that the modern world puts to the church. Indeed it is extremely difficult for the church to affirm itself with total conviction before such a threatening world, but nothing less is required. The world has a way of overturning the plans of the church, revealing its weaknesses, taking away its prestige, destroying the confidence of people who put their hopes in it. Yet it is precisely in this capacity that the world serves a memorial function in the church, never allowing the church to mistake itself for the fully achieved kingdom of God and forever reminding it of its vocation to humble service.

Prophetic Function

The world exercises another vital function in and for the church by way of challenge and provocation —a prophetic function. If it is true that the church is sometimes tempted to forget its divine election and grace-given character, it can also be tempted, when remembering it, to regard this election as a declaration of divine favor that restricts God's love and presence to itself. The fact that universal grace has never been taken too seriously by the church is but one indication that it has not altogether resisted this temptation. An exclusivist understanding of the Covenant has always allured the people of God: The Lord is "their" God and they are "his" people. Lest there be any misunderstanding, the world raises its prophetic voice and challenges the church to discover the active presence of God in the world. Thus the church is made to realize that even on its own, the world is not God-forsaken, completely abandoned, and without grace.

Indeed not everything in the world is merely defection from God and opposition to God's will. There is in the world genuine love of neighbor, hunger for justice and peace, personal integrity, struggle for truth and liberation. Does it not come as a prophetic surprise to Christians that the civil rights movement, the peace movements, the hunger and poverty crusades, the anti-war demonstrations, and many other areas of expected Christian concern are often being initiated and led by secular humanists? Is not the church provoked to greater involvement in the plight of the poor and the misery of the oppressed when it sees its worldly partner sometimes scoring more points both for concern and for efficiency?

Insofar as the church accepts the challenge of our

times, it proves its vitality and shapes its future.
When it ignores the prophetic voice of the world, it
in a sense passes judgment on itself and raises
questions with regard to its relevancy. The prophetic role of the world consists mainly in lifting Christians out of their feeling of impotence and superflu-
ousness, which derives from the self-defeating impression that the new world is being built up without them. History records a number of secular
prophets who have played an indispensable part in
spurring the church toward reforming action. They
have all disturbed the established security of the
church, and not infrequently they have been taken
for enemies. Indeed it is not surprising that the
prophetic voice with which the world begins to
speak to the church is not always welcome. The
daring resistance of the worldly prophet has often
gone against intolerable situations and objection-
able practices in the church, and its rebukes have
been sharp. Yet it remains, for all that, a striking
example of the sovereign liberty of the Holy Spirit,
who works where and when he will.

Although obviously the world is not called to that
specific function in saving history for which the
church alone is chosen, we have seen nonetheless
that it has a multifarious function to exercise in the
church. It may be objected that the world is hardly
ever conscious of any such role or influence and
consequently is an unlikely brother in partnership.
The truth of the matter is, however, that brothers
need not be conscious of their real solidarity; they

simply stand together in the reality of life. The most genuine fraternal services that brothers render unto one another are not necessarily those which are based on explicit communication, nor are they necessarily those which are best understood or appreciated. Generally speaking, the unspoken and undeclared signs of loyalty and affection between brothers are the sincerest and often the most rewarding. If this is true of ordinary brothers, it is eminently true of the church and the world, which God has united in the divine brotherhood of Christ.

6

Evangelization and Development

Never before have the claims on Christianity been so great. The world expects the Christian churches to become totally committed to development. It expects them not only to sensitize their people to the formidable challenges of development and offer an authoritative opinion as to what is to be done, but also to divert an ever increasing amount of their resources to works of development.

The first question, therefore, is whether or not the church can honestly live up to these expectations and demands. Is it not asking and expecting too much from the church? Is social involvement of this magnitude the proper task of the church? It can of course be argued that Jesus himself was no helper of society on a grand scale. He did relieve a number of individuals from sickness, but he did not deal with all the sick, even in one particular district, nor did he create some sort of organization to conquer illnesses. He multiplied bread on one or two occasions, but he did not feed the hungry generally. He made no apparent effort to bridge the gap between the poor and the rich of his day. Bad administration, poor housing conditions, bad roads, inadequate water supplies were not his concern. Yet these social evils were certainly not lacking in his day. Moreover, the gospel he preached did not contain any social program.

It can also be argued, perhaps more convincingly, that the church is not in fact a master problem-solver, as though Christians possessed some sort of secret formula or magic wand for development. Christian faith does offer some directive guidance about the origin, meaning, and destiny of the world, but this does not mean that the church has all the answers to today's problems—let alone all the valid questions. It cannot hand down specific solutions to social and political problems from the pulpit. When it comes to human development, the church receives from divine revelation no light other than that of all people and their experiences. This means that Christians have to search tentatively for solutions like everyone else, since the pattern and solutions for development are no clearer for them than for non-Christians.

These preliminary remarks are meant as a warning. We must not try to attribute more to the people of God than they are capable of fulfilling. The church cannot solve the agonizing problems thrown up by the world today—neither the problem of hunger, nor population, nor race hatred, nor unemployment, nor underdevelopment. This is a sobering thought, perhaps a disappointing perspective, to begin with. However, it does point to something very positive and constructive: The church and the world are indeed partners in life and for life. If development is achieved, it will never be to the sole credit of Christians, even were they all to start working together for development tomorrow. On the other hand, if development is not achieved, Christians will not be entirely to blame. Development will either be a joint success, a shared victory between the church and the world, or it will be a joint failure. Since they are co-partners, the church and the world are co-responsible for development. The church must therefore link its own search, a search in faith, with the search of humankind for solutions to the specific problems of development. This immediately raises a serious question for the church.

The Dilemma

The dilemma facing the church today, particularly in mission countries, can be formulated in the following way: Which duty should be given precedence, evangelization or development? The present crisis in the missionary vocation is generally experienced in terms of precedence or priority and the inevitable failure to establish a correct relationship between evangelization and development. On the one hand, there are those missionaries who feel that it is impossible to preach the gospel without having first fed one's hungry listeners, without having first satisfied their basic human needs in matters such as housing, education, and medical care. Hence many missionaries do find themselves almost completely absorbed in humanitarian and cultural tasks. They feel that in the long run it is better to give wholehearted and unstinted support to development and thus help the poor attain something approaching a decent human life. The real danger here is not that these missionaries have put themselves so squarely behind the cause of development that evangelization has become in practice a secondary aim in their ministry, but that they have not been able to do this with a perfectly clear conscience. Their qualms of conscience are made worse by the grave misgivings of their superiors and other missionary colleagues who feel they are going too far afield and neglecting evangelization.

On the other hand, there are other missionaries who insist on the unyielding primacy of evangelization and are reluctant to become seriously involved in development. In the newly independent countries of the Third World, where the winds of development are beginning to blow at gale proportions, even these dedicated missionaries are starting to have second thoughts about their missionary commitment. Those working in Africa, for example, still feel the resentment and deep-cutting criticism of African Christian leaders who reproach the church for not having done all it could to support the independence movement that swept over Africa in the mid-fifties. Not wishing to repeat past mistakes, these same missionaries are beginning to question seriously their present priorities. Already their timidity and slowness in putting their weight resolutely behind the cause of development is coming increasingly under attack by the new governments.

This dilemma is not resolved, nor is the anxiety of the missionaries allayed, simply by reiterating the obvious fact that both works must be carried out at the same time and that it is not a question of either/or. As people of action, they want to know how this comprehensive approach is to be achieved in practice. While it is certainly true that evangelization invariably leads to involvement in the social and political problems of society and that the gospel must also promote the temporal welfare of people everywhere, the practical problem of correlating evangelization and development effectively still remains unresolved. Little is gained by insisting that in theory the two are not mutually exclusive, but complementary. The missionaries' everyday lives and experiences have long taught them this axiomatic truth and any further attempt to convince them of it would be superfluous. What they are not so clear about is the way in which they are to pursue these two aims simultaneously and successfully. In the down-to-earth realities of missionary life, they know better than any theologian how these two giants do in fact collide, antagonize, interfere with and at times even work against one another. More often than not, evangelization and development appear in the missionary context as two bulls in the same pasture, both vying for supremacy. When and if a *modus vivendi* is achieved, it is usually at the expense of separating the two bulls and allowing them to graze in clearly fenced-off areas. The result is a tenuous coexistence in which evangelization and development are given to run a parallel course alongside one another with a minimal amount of contact and interference. And so the dilemma remains. Either missionaries feel torn away from evangelization by their heavy "mortar-and-cement" commitment to development, or else they feel that they are neglecting development by promoting the so-called primary task of the church.

It is my firm conviction that as long as the problem is posed in terms of precedence or priority (whether on the doctrinal level or the pastoral level), the frustration and perplexity in the hearts of so many missionaries will only increase. We can readily indicate the nature of this problem by a close analogy. The traditional Catholic doctrine on marriage has, until recently, enshrined—not to say canonized—the distinction between primary and secondary ends of marriage. The position is well known. The primary and essential purpose of marriage, intended by God, was said to be the procreation and upbringing of offspring. No other primary purpose could be maintained. The secondary purposes were mutual help and the allaying of or lawful outlet for concupiscence. These secondary purposes could not stand on the same level as the first, but rather were said to be essentially subordinate to it. Today there is a clear rejection of this hierarchically arranged triad of purposes so dominant in the older theology of marriage. In place of it there is an ever increasing stress upon conjugal love as a higher, more Christian, integrating principle of married life.

Similarly, we must reject the traditional attempt to correlate evangelization and development in terms of primary and secondary ends of the church. All such attempts lead to a practical impasse and only protract the present missionary crisis in the church. What is needed is a new definition of the mission of the church, one which subsumes and integrates evangelization and development according to a higher principle. We strongly suggest that any new missionary synthesis will have to take universal grace seriously into account—not because it is an easier option, but because it is the heart of every missionary endeavor and ultimately defines the specific mission of the church itself.

The theology of universal grace outlined in this book provides, we feel, the only valid basis whereby the pressing dilemma between evangelization and development can be resolved. When universal grace is given its rightful place in the doctrine and ministry of the church, it becomes the integrating principle of a new synthesis and a better understanding of the church. Universal grace becomes, as it were, the kingbolt by which the forward axle and wheels of development and the chassis of evangeli-

zation are objectively connected and made to function unto the same end. Evangelization and development are both transcended. They are no longer
seen as two separate and quite distinct spheres of
missionary activity, as though time and Christian
energy given to one were time and energy stolen
from the other. Universal grace assures the church
that all powers and potentialities of development,
together with those of evangelization, can—indeed
must—be made subservient to the ultimate goal of
furthering humanity in Christ.

Because they *can* be made subservient the church
should not be afraid to join forces with non-Christians in freeing all the potential in people, knowing,
as it does so, that this very liberation includes the
real possibility of recognizing and responding to
God's word. Because they *must* be subservient, neither development nor evangelization can ever be
given priority over the other, as though one were
somehow more crucial than the other; or still,
worse, as though one could be construed simply as
a means, a preparatory stage, for the other.

The Church's Mission

So far we have been considering the dilemma facing
the church and have indicated that its mission must
be properly and directly defined in relation to universal grace. It is now time for a closer look at this
definition. One might say that the whole life and
mission of the church—initially as well as ulti-

mately—lies in its power to see the invisible and to build upon "what no man has ever seen," namely, the grace of God universally present in the world and in the hearts of all people. It is first of all in seeing, recognizing, and encountering Christ at the heart of every human existence that the church is able, under its own faithful eyes, to unfold what there is to be seen. In the domain of faith, which is the proper and direct sphere of mission, there is an intrinsic correlation between the power to see and the unfolding of what there is to be seen. Thus the church must first of all develop ever more perfect eyes so that there will always be something more to be seen. If the renewal of the church is primarily the result of gazing upon Christ, the renewal of humankind by the church can only be achieved by gazing on Christ where he *already* is, in the hearts of all people and in all the realities of the world. Hence the mission of the church is emphatically one of discernment. Like the disciples of Emmaus, the essential missionary experience of the church must always be the recognition of Christ, who joins company ever so unobtrusively and walks alongside the church.

This recognition of Christ, which is the church's essential role in the world, necessarily involves risk. For the disciples of Emmaus, it meant the risk of hoping against hope; for doubting Thomas, the risk of faith; for the other disciples it meant letting their despair be dispersed and their whole subsequent lives be transformed. For them all it was the meaning and fulfillment of their lives that was at stake. Similarly, if the church is to carry out its mission in the world, it must be prepared to take the risk of "recognizing" Christ wherever he is and under whatever form he may appear. And the church is to do this, moreover, in the firm conviction that the success of its mission lies in the ventures that Christ is forever making on its behalf, involving the risk of not being recognized by his own friends.

In this view, the church's mission does not consist in bringing Christ to the world: having been sent by his heavenly Father, Christ not only comes continually to the world, but through the Spirit he is at work *where* he wills and *when* he wills. It is the church's task to recognize Christ at work and to preach the good news of this recognition to the poor. Its mission consists essentially in proclaiming the acceptable year of the Lord. In this it participates in the mission of the Holy Spirit, without whose light it is impossible to recognize Christ and exclaim, like the disciple whom Jesus loved: "It is the Lord!" For the church, mission means, above all, this: that behind the phenomena of the world and within them the Face of the Lord is encountered and recognized; and thus his saving presence is made known in the history of the world.

It will be evident that this definition of mission will deeply affect our understanding of the church's role in evangelization and development. First of all, evangelization: to "evangelize" people can only

mean to help them *realize* that Jesus is really the
heart of the world and of their own lives. In a strict
sense evangelization, whatever way it is done, is
always the revelation to people through the church
of Jesus Christ in whom people are already living
—hence the revelation of their "universal brother."
From all that we have said about universal grace, it
is evident that the process of evangelization does
not mean to announce or bring the supernatural as
something foreign to human nature, for through
the effects of the Incarnation human nature is already permeated with the grace of Christ. Evangelization consists mainly in the act of recognizing this
inherited grace-fullness and thus liberating the
universal grace inherent in the world's own saved
human existence. In other words, the church is
entrusted with the task of bringing to light our
universal brotherhood in Christ and, like the Master himself, stirring up an "I-Thou" relationship
through the sacramental hem of its visible garment.

We see a confirmation of the Lord's antecedent
presence in the world and in every human being in
the proclamation of the gospel and the way people
respond to it. It is because people exist in Christ
even now, in the depths of their personal being,
that they can freely accept the good news proclaimed by the church. Indeed it is because the Lord
is already present and active in the world that the
church has a mission at all, that it can and must
proclaim him from the housetops. For this proclamation is successful only because its hearers are

capable of accepting it for what it really is—the word of God. Such a capacity—which must be God-given—would indicate that grace is already somehow present in the hearts of people even before the church reaches them.

It would be an error to suppose that grace is granted only at the moment when the preaching of the gospel reaches the auditor. If, at that moment, grace becomes especially moving and efficacious, it is because it has been there all the time as a kind of grace in existence itself. Thus the invisible appearance of the Lord always precedes his outward appearance and recognition. It has been said that in all his dealings and encounters with people, the Lord works from the inside outwards. What he begins in "mystery" eventually breaks through in epiphany." This is certainly true of evangelization. The insight issuing in the believers' initial response to the word of God always comes as an "outbreak" of grace, an emergence or birth, and consequently as the epiphany of grace already present in human hearts.

One would not be very far off the mark in saying that evangelization is basically what Socrates would call a maieutic process and the church's role that of a midwife. Through evangelization the church assists the world in giving birth to the Christ-life ever anew. The church must elicit and gently draw out the universal grace that is latent in humankind, thereby giving increasing form and figure to Christ in the world. The proclamation of the gospel is never in vain since it is essentially the good news that the acceptable time of the Lord has come, that *now* is the hour of deliverance.

To some, our observations might seem to diminish the importance of the evangelization of non-Christians. If all people indeed belong to Christ before having been reached by the church's proclamation, why must missionaries make all their efforts and sacrifice themselves and maybe even their lives to bring them the gospel? After all, what good is it to preach what I believe to people if they already live what I desire to reveal to them? Does not the viewpoint we have taken with respect to universal grace reduce the urgency of evangelization, of explicit faith, of the work of conversions? There is a danger that some readers might hastily conclude that the missionary task of the church is thereby rendered superfluous—and certainly not the essential mission confided to the church by Christ himself. Nothing could be further from the truth, and this for a variety of reasons that we shall presently examine.

Nevertheless there is this to be said: To the extent that historically the urgency of mission has been based on the fear that without the church pagans and other non-Christians would be left without grace and without Christ, such an underlying motivation seems in retrospect to have been misguided. While it was perhaps immediately successful in increasing the number of converts, it is no longer justifiable today for that reason alone. Although the

apostolic zeal of the church can never be ques-
tioned—indeed it can never be sufficiently
promoted—the motives whereby it seeks to support and sustain its missionary efforts are always
subject to re-examination in the light of historical
developments.

We must stress that what we are suggesting here
in no way diminishes the importance or urgency of
mission. On the contrary, evangelization will retain
its true meaning only if the church situates itself
rightly before the mystery of universal grace: Then
the question of urgency becomes all the more compelling. For if, on the one hand, all people find
themselves in a state of original grace—that is, if
they are radically related to Christ and he to them
—and if, on the other hand, his hour of deliverance
has come, then it becomes all the more imperative
for the church to be present and assist at this "new
birth," wherever and whenever it may be taking
place. Even though all people may have conceived
the Lord in their hearts, they have not all brought
the Christ-life to birth. Without the proper assistance and ministry of the church there is every danger of a miscarriage and the real possibility of this
grace coming to naught. But given the church's
loving attention and solicitous care, and especially
its depth of sensitivity to the authentic presence of
Christ, this embryonic grace will be able to develop
and, with time and sacramental care, become "fully
mature with the fulness of Christ himself" (Eph.
4:13). This means that the act of evangelization

primarily consists in the church's power to discern God's action in people, to reveal and clarify it for them, and to help them turn decisively toward God in achieving their life project. The church does this, above all, by confessing its own faith, by exposing to the non-Christian its own relation to Christ and testifying to the ultimate meaning it has discerned, for itself, in relationship with Christ. Only when such a witness is cradled in evangelization is it possible for non-Christians to see that our Christian faith concerns them as well and that Christ's love truly lies at the heart of their own lives.

Charity and Development

We must now turn our attention to the problem of development. As indicated earlier, the problem is a pressing one for missionaries in countries where poverty and social injustice are rife. Yet, when universal grace is seen as the hitherto missing link between evangelization and development, that is, as the integrating principle of a new missionary outlook, much of the difficulty and misunderstanding is removed. Before pursuing our investigations further, however, it is important to know what is meant by development and how it differs from charity. It is hardly possible to make a study on the question with which we are concerned without a consensus on the meaning of these two important words.

If it is true that development is the new name for peace, as has been suggested in modern times, it does not follow that charity is another name for development. Although both can and should coalesce in the liberating power of practical action, it would be a mistake simply to equate the two or to blur the difference between them, as church people are so often prone to do. In their eagerness to prove that the church has always worked for development, many point to the numerous church-sponsored works such as schools, hospitals, dispensaries. Indeed, mission stations have even been likened to the medieval Benedictine abbey which, alongside (!) its church, often had a school, a dispensary, a guest-house, and a farm. It is usually on this basis that missionaries are said to have always been involved in development. The fact of the matter is, however, that such a conclusion can most euphemistically be called hasty. It is true that "pure evangelization," in a disembodied form, has never existed; it is equally true that the church has generally regarded development in terms of real, human assistance to the poor. But it does not follow that *works of charity* are the same as *action for development*.

Giving clothes to the naked, food to the hungry, medicine to the sick, and shelter to the homeless are works of charity, not actions for development. Charitable works (whatever their form) will always be necessary, will always exist in the church, and will always be a sign of Christ's love for people. The old story of the Good Samaritan will always be one of the better models of the church's spirituality. The compassion and mercy of the church is unmistakenly channelled in one direction: the service of humankind, of every condition, in every weakness and need, but particularly the poor, the exploited, the hungry, the dependent, the displaced, the disenfranchised, and the most abandoned. Hence the church has never had to fear working itself out of a job as long as one person, let alone hundreds of millions, remained hungry, unwanted, unloved. It must be recognized, however, that the action of the Good Samaritan was an act of mercy and not a work of development. The difference between the two is noteworthy.

First, an act of charity is always made in the present and for the present, that is, unto the needful person who presents himself to me, here and now, as *my* neighbor. Charity is always directed to a real neighbor rather than to a possible neighbor, whereas action for development, while not excluding the real person of today, looks more to the future—the future betterment of a country, a people, a generation. When we work for development, we work more for our children and the upcoming generation than for our immediate contemporaries. Development is a process, often a long process. It is like planting a tree, the fruits of which will come in abundance only at a much later date. In other words, what we sow in development is reaped more especially by those who come after us. Charity is mindful of the present, whereas development is future-oriented. The former springs from an immediately personal love, the latter from a singularly collective hope.

Without hope, there can be no self-help, no self-determination, and no self-development. There can be no collective incentive or national will to build roads, irrigate fields, stop land erosion, save money, and provide fresh water supplies in villages. Hope is the bedrock of development. Hence the first major contribution to development must be to foster, generate, and maintain hope in development prospects and projects: hope that an apparently hopeless situation can be changed; hope that human hands do in fact contain the energy and strength to change the face of the earth. It is in this area that the church is particularly well-qualified to make a vital contribution: to arouse people out of their inner apathy and encourage them to become self-reliant. Yet such a task requires much more than an occasional exhortation from the pulpit and certainly more than a spurious "pilot project" undertaken on or near the mission grounds. In fact, it will make heavy demands on every moral fiber of the church's being and tax its best concerted efforts to the utmost.

Second, charity is above all characterized by spontaneity and promptness. At its best, charity does not calculate, make plans, or set priorities. The Samaritan's conduct is particularly revealing here. He acted without hesitating, without even thinking of the Law or trying to find out who was the object of his care. His compassion welled up spontaneously and, unlike the priest and the Levite who halted for a moment without knowing what to do, he promptly aided the wretched man. Nor does charity plan its encounters any more than did the Samaritan. Such needful encounters arise unexpectedly; they seem to just "happen," any time of the day or night, often when we least expect or desire them. This fortuitous element is precisely what gives charity its unique beauty as a spontaneous, unreflecting reaction of love. Charity is best characterized by that inner readiness to let anyone in need enter our lives unannounced, unsolicited, and quite independently of that person's lovableness. In this it differs considerably from development, which of necessity requires reflection, planning, and organization.

It might be argued that planning at times does go into Christian charity as, for example, when money, medicine, and food supplies are collected on a grand scale and sent by church organizations to disaster areas or poverty-stricken countries. But this is relief work rather than development. And relief is simply a more organized form of charity which is raised from the individual level to that of the larger Christian body. Relief is primarily aimed at alleviating the more immediately critical needs of a people in distress, whereas development seeks to eradicate the causes that give rise to these needs. Like our Good Samaritan, charity thinks of taking a dying man to the nearest hospital and, if necessary, picks up the medical bill. Development, on the other hand, would be more concerned about the safety conditions of the road down from Jerusalem to

Jericho and would do all it could to prevent similar occurrences. A mission hospital, therefore, can be rightly considered as a work of development only to the extent that it incorporates preventive medicine and a serious training and health program.

There is a third factor that, in practice, often differentiates charity from development. Whereas charity can, and sometimes does, make the recipient or subject dependent upon the donor, development never does. Since the first and foremost concern of real development is to promote self-reliance, not only are the subjects of development emphatically discouraged from coming back "for more of the same," but they are spared even the temptation of such a parasitic attitude. It is becoming apparent today that much of the church's charity in the past, particularly in the missions, was not altogether disinterested and completely free of that kind of possessive love which makes more for dependence than real liberation. Love of neighbor must not aim at any ulterior purpose, even a religious or missionary purpose. This is the meaning of the parable of the Good Samaritan who, after attending to the needs of the half-dead stranger, goes his way without even wondering how the story will end. True charity is disinterested, without strings attached.

A further cautionary remark is called for here. However illuminating the parable of the Good Samaritan may be, it does not tell us everything about Christian charity. Hence there is a danger that we shall come to think of charity almost exclusively in terms of pouring oil over the sufferings of destitute people. Loving one's neighbor would mean only alleviating the cares and sorrows of others. Such a lopsided vision of charity is still very common among Christians. No single person in modern times has done more to correct this faulty vision than Teilhard de Chardin, who views charity within the larger framework of the cosmos and asks: "Does it not also imply that out of an active sympathy we should spend ourselves on behalf of the great body of mankind, not merely to heal its wounds but to participate in all its hopes and fears and in building it up in line with what creation demands?" In this perspective, charity becomes the driving force of development. Without ceasing to be compassionate, charity finds its highest expression in Christians committing their whole lives to the cause of integral development and to the full realization of what it is to be human.

This is where we see that the objective purpose of evangelization and development is to create a new person. With universal grace as a common denominator, as a Christic *substratum*, evangelization and development participate in the same liberating process of humankind that extends, without discontinuity, from the possession of what people need to communion with the Lord, the goal of all history. Since even the material world has within itself a divine force that transcends the realm of the merely contingent, any and every effort that promotes the world's perfection and liberates people in the face of oppression advances the plan and kingdom of God, which will last forever. By its genuine efforts in this process of liberation, whether through evangelization or development, the church objectively prepares for that consummation by which God will transform our universe into a real community of peace, a new heaven and a new earth. Since the grace of God is universally present and operative in the world, evangelization and development are transcended and both find their ultimate meaning in the words of Christ: "I have come that they may have life and have it in abundance" (John 10:10).

Liberation

There are several models that can be used to interpret the common objective of evangelization and development, but the concept of *liberation* has decided advantages. It reflects the real meaning and the urgency of both. It is a notion that also accomodates easily to areas other than the economic and sociopolitical. It is an excellent vehicle for synthesizing the false polarities of creation and redemption, nature and grace. Furthermore, not only is liberation particularly meaningful in this, our "second development decade," but it is also a prominent and central theme of the Bible.

In the Bible, liberation is not a once-mentioned theme; rather it occurs repeatedly as the central theme of salvation history itself. God's election of a people is inseparable from the liberating event of Exodus. By delivering Israel from Egyptian bondage and uniting kin and families in a sacred covenant on the basis of that deliverance, God reveals himself as the author of justice, the God of the oppressed, involved in their history, liberating them from human bondage.

This event impressed the national Israelite consciousness as the basis and determining act for all time of God's self-disclosure. In this remarkable liberation was to be learned more clearly than anywhere else what God willed and what God was all about. Hence, in all that happened subsequently, the Israelites simply interpreted the meaning of events in the light of this "passover." The prophets would remind them that the kind of religious observance that pleases God is "to break unjust fetters and undo the thongs of the yoke, to let the oppressed go free and break every yoke" (Isa. 58:6). They would consistently speak of God's concern for the lack of social, economic, and political justice for the poor, the unwanted, and the unloved in the community. The kingdom of peace that they announced supposed the establishment of justice, defense of the rights of the poor, punishment of the oppressor, a life without fear of being enslaved. The theme of liberation was taken up and reaffirmed by Jesus himself who came "to proclaim liberty to captives and to set the oppressed free" (Luke 4:18). To suggest that Jesus was concerned only about the "spiritual" liberation of people, that is, one that does not affect unjust conditions and social structures, is to overlook completely Jesus' Hebrew view of the person, which ignores the body-soul dichotomy.

If liberation is one of the key concepts of salvation history, it is also the new name for development and evangelization. In either context, it directly refers to the quality of life of people living in communion with one another. Liberation is primarily a problem of justice, and the peculiarity of justice is that it directs people in their relations with others and thus besets them at their spiritual core. As Berdyaev said, "Care for the life of another, even material bodily care, is spiritual in essence. Bread for myself is a material question; bread for my neighbor is a spiritual question." What gives development and evangelization their supreme liberating value is that both are a permanent effort of justice. Therefore, since personal sin embodies itself in unjust and enslaving structures, and since Christ is the supreme liberator, then clearly the church's main task is one of liberation, and clearly this means from *all* enslavements—both its roots in sin and its appearance in unjust human structures. The two are inseparable. For only when all the frustrated aspirations, the stifled abilities, and the latent potentialities of humankind are set free, only when universal grace is liberated and brought to fruition, will all things be restored and hold together in Christ.

7

Future Prospects of the Church in Africa

So far we have dealt with three salient issues: (1) the common denominator of grace that makes Christians and non-Christians brothers and sisters to one another, (2) the fraternal partnership between the church and the world, and (3) the substratum of grace that must be taken into account in evangelization and development. We now come to the question of the church's future prospects in developing countries, and Africa is chosen for our discussion. In every instance, what we have said has been sharply refracted through the prism of universal grace. This is very important also as we try to see what the future holds in store for the church in Africa, for in this and other developing areas events will be shaped by whether or not universal grace is taken with the seriousness required. In short, the church will have to be particularly sensitive to those areas where God is on the move; having learned where they are, it must make all possible haste to be there with him. The question before us is: "Will the church have a significant future in the New Africa of tomorrow?" At least four legitimate approaches or ways we can attempt to answer this question are open to us.

Evaluation Approach

The first approach would consist in evaluating the weakness and strength of the church in Africa at the coming of national independence. In the same way that one judges a man's prospects for the future on the basis of his past performance, one could legitimately try to predict the church's future on the grounds of its past shortcomings and achievements. Using this criterion, the Christian church would at first sight seem to have been in a strong position when the African colonial territories stood poised, by the mid-1950s, on the brink of independence.

In the credit column, one would find many encouraging signs, not the least of which being that the church had proved itself to be a people's movement in Africa. It was not a movement restricted to the small elite of national leaders or the wider elite of the schooled. Covering the widest social spectrum, it included rich and poor, illiterate and literate, cabinet ministers and truck drivers, mechanical engineers and ordinary farmers. People from all walks of life were able, at least here, to rub elbows without any social distinction.

Another factor which was very much to the church's credit was its signal contribution to education. It may not have been the best education, but it was a remarkable beginning of mental discipline, intellectual honesty, and moral courage. Moreover, it did answer a strongly felt need of the people to be able to read and write in their own language. Here statistics are particularly revealing. By 1963, for example, there were 1,049 primary schools in Lesotho (at that time Basutoland). Only six of these were provided by the colonial government; the rest were sponsored and run by the missions: Paris Evangelical (448), Roman Catholic (437), Anglican (138), other (16). This was the general school pattern throughout Africa. Of all the recognized schools in British Africa, even as early as 1923, six thousand were mission schools and only one hundred were government schools. In the Belgian Congo the proportion was roughly the same. Hence it is easy to understand why all the mistakes in African education were made by missionaries: Since they were virtually the only people engaged in formal education, they were the only ones who could make mistakes. In the eyes of the African people, however, the benefits of this first education far outweighed its shortcomings.

In the credit column, one would also have to add the church's care for the sick and the needy: dispensaries, maternity clinics, mission hospitals, leprosaria, and relief programs. The church has always been mindful of the most sorely afflicted and for this reason was firmly rooted in the hearts of many Africans. Even though organized Christianity had professed a primary concern for souls, it never entirely neglected the stark poverty that damns them, the economic conditions that stifle their initiative, or the social conditions that cripple them. The church did, after a fashion, minister to the "whole" person. Moreover, the Christian life of faith did afford Africans a new spiritual experience that was real and vital. Ordinary men and women did experience the power of Christ at work in their lives.

Yet it is also true that in the mid-fifties ominous signs were beginning to appear and deep-cutting criticisms were beginning to be heard. Against the contention that the church was a people's movement came the criticism that the church was not doing all it could to promote the Independence movement then sweeping Africa. In the light of its claim for justice and respect for the individual, the church was expected to do more. Another weakness in the eyes of the Africans was the church's lack of conviction in the practice of racial equality. Its failure to speak out loud and clear against racial discrimination was interpreted quite naturally as the silence of approval and consent. Still another weakness of the church—one that many African Christians now regard as the most crucial—was its slowness in becoming a truly African church, both in worship and theological thinking.

There was also the church's heavy dependence on funds and personnel from overseas. With the

convenient crutch of outside aid, it is painfully obvious that the church was not in fact as strong as it
appeared to be. The umbilical life-line with the
mother churches in western countries would have
to be severed sooner or later. As long as the funds
did continue to pour in, they were controlled by the
expatriate missionaries. And here as elsewhere,
"He who pays the piper calls the tune." Although
the church did develop and prosper, its strength
was too often calculated in terms of prestige and
power. As a result, it is not surprising that when
confronted with the delicate task of working out
new church-state relations in the years following
independence, both sides experienced grave misgivings, tension, and intimidation. It can be readily
seen that the evaluation of the church's past
strength and weakness, while profitable because
instructive, does not satisfactorily resolve the question of its future prospects on the African continent.
Not only does the weakness of the church neutral-
ize—in terms of prognostication—its strength for
the future, but the demands and needs of the future
will be entirely different. In order to meet them, the
church will have to call upon different resources of
imagination and inner strength.

   If we turn now to the assets and liabilities of the
church in the immediate present, the prospects of
its future appear even more problematic. On the
positive side, one cannot fail to be impressed by the
large number of Christians who attend church services in what often amounts to standing room only.

Not only are the churches full, but new converts are daily coming into the Christian community. Indeed the rapid and widespread growth in adherents of the Christian faith throughout Africa in this century has been unparalleled in the twenty centuries of the church's history. This phenomenal growth, which continues unabated today, would strongly suggest that the church does have a future in Africa. The Reverend Dr. B. Barrett, an expert on African statistics, predicts that within the foreseeable future the Christian population of Africa will reach some 350 million, as compared with the present total of about 74 million. These figures give weight to the perhaps remote and seemingly far-fetched conjecture that the preponderant Christian center of influence and interest will inevitably shift from Europe and the northern part of the American continent to Africa.

While not without its merits, such a futuristic vision goes well beyond what we would safely consider a plausible working hypothesis. True, the rapid increase of Christians on the African continent is still gaining momentum, and the numbers will probably soar in the next ten years. The numerical strength of the church is growing, but is its influence? The situation in Latin America sorely reminds us that statistics can be a misleading yardstick when it comes to gauging the real presence and significance of the church. History also tells us that in the long run Christianity has never been at its best following a sudden, uncontrolled landslide of new members.

What makes the growth rate of the church so problematic in the present situation is the parallel and equally staggering rate of urbanization in Africa and the fact that the church is conspicuously absent from this urban concentration. It is conservatively estimated that 25 million Africans now live in urban areas, with another million added every year. What statistics do not tell us is the appalling rate at which the young Africans living in these cities, especially those under twenty-five, are deserting the church. Their defection is as unobstrusive as it is unannounced; yet it has already reached alarming exodus proportions. Having drifted from the countryside into amorphously growing towns that are poor, dirty, and overcrowded, the half-educated and unemployed youth shed their religion—if not their faith altogether—with disarming ease and frequency. Their former Christian pattern of life slides swiftly away from them, like snow off a roof. What is perhaps even more disconcerting is the fact that the church has not yet begun to give serious attention to the migrants, still less to the problems of African youth in the world of the city. The success of the church in Africa has been, and to a large extent still is, almost exclusively restricted to the rural, more traditional, bush areas. Here the majority of the missionaries spend their lives: overworked, dispersing their efforts over a wide field, visiting innumerable outstations, bush schools, and groups of Christians who would otherwise be left entirely on their own. While this missionary effort is admirable and undoubtedly fruitful far beyond our human estimates, nonetheless one wonders how much of it is expended in vain. For much of what the church initially gains in these remote areas is subsequently lost in the neglected urban areas. What the church picks up with one hand, it drops with the other. What first appeared as a promising harvest soon turns out to be a rather mediocre yield.

Another factor which neutralizes the numerical success of the church in Africa is that missionary enthusiasm has grown exceedingly temperate. Under much better living conditions and with larger communities of Christians to care for, many missionaries look back to the labor of the earlier pioneering years with nostalgia —almost as to a lost era of innocence. This tempering of enthusiasm is found not only among the African clergy, who never really understood or shared the feverish sense of urgency of their white colleagues, but also and especially among the expatriate missionaries who still constitute a two-thirds majority in many areas. The reason for the latter's diminishing missionary thrust is understandable. On the one hand, there is the question of age. The number of expatriate missionaries fifty years of age or over who are still on duty is considerable. A man over fifty cannot serve, as he perhaps once could, several thousand Christians scattered over a "parish" that is often as large as one or more European countries. He just hasn't the physical strength. With increasing opportunities thus slipping through his fingers unfulfilled, he is threatened with a loss of nerve; he has no peace, no quiet, and no time. On the other hand, not only do the expatriate missionaries feel powerless, but they are also experiencing a growing sense of self-estrangement. Feeling foreign among a group of strangers is quite understandable, but feeling out of place in the midst of those with whom one has lived, worked, and identified for so many missionary years can be a harrowing experience.

This sense of alienation is brought on partly by the fact that the very Christians who once treated them with veneration and obedience are becoming more and more critical and exigent. It is also caused by the scarcely hidden feelings of their African co-missioners who would gladly dispense with the foreigners' unfriendly scrutiny and awkward company. Before coming to the missions, the expatriate missionaries were told that one of their primary tasks was to prepare an indigenous clergy and thus eventually work themselves out of a job. Like a good teacher, they were to render themselves superfluous. This sound advice was accepted readily enough then, especially since the prospect of its ever happening in their own missionary lifetime was indeed remote. Today, in many missions, the situation has changed drastically. All of a sudden —or so it would appear to many of them—they are being asked to assume a supporting role rather than a leading role. In fact, they have already handed over many posts and responsibilities to Africans.

But it is one thing to step down graciously, and quite another thing to adjust psychologically to an entirely new situation after so many years. This shift of power comes hard on expatriate missionaries who not only were taken by surprise at the speed of localization but never took kindly to the idea of localization at all. So many feel prematurely retired—at least from an important sphere of human activity and control—as well as feeling that they are destined to disappear and become extinct, like the dinosaurs of old.

For all these reasons it is doubtful whether the future is as bright for the church as statistics would have us believe. In any event, the evaluation approach has not proved sufficiently conclusive and we are therefore obliged to consider another approach to our exercise of prophecy.

Problematic Approach

In a changing, developing Africa, where planning and looking ahead is not only important but necessary for survival, the question of the church's future in Africa may be worded in yet another way: If the church can look ahead, plan, and readjust itself to these plans, it should normally survive and have a significant future.

No one will deny that in our time we are witnessing a new way of speaking about the future, a way that is matter-of-fact, scientific, and above all necessary. Planning is certainly indispensable for a fu-

ture which cannot be waited for in sheer passivity.
Thus the large number of surveyors, planners, ad-
visers, consultants, and co-ordinators actually engaged in developing countries is not a luxury but a
necessity. Whether on the national or international
level, planning has become the hallmark of our age
and the sign par excellence of our times—family
planning, city planning, economic and development planning, etc. Indeed, social life is fundamentally the maintenance and organization of the
future. As Mounier said, "Only those who envisage
man's future are qualified to decipher the mysteries
of living man."

Planning is also one of the great challenges of the
church in developing countries. In the past, mission planning was either nonexistent or haphazard.
The missionaries thrived like pioneers and trail
blazers; they were doers, not planners. They took
things in their stride and adjusted themselves to
whatever situation arose. In fact, this energetic
promptness and capacity for instantly grasping an
unexpected situation accounts for the church's vitality and growth in those early years. Had they
been more cautious, calculating, and bent on im-
plementing a preconceived plan of action, it is
doubtful whether they would have accomplished
as much. While this venturesome approach did
have its advantages in pioneering days, it can no
longer be justified, nor will it be tolerated much
longer by the African governments.

The success of the church is obviously not de-

termined by statistics and planning if these are understood superficially. The mystery of the future is
more than the realization of plans made today. Yet,
planning is not unrelated to obedience to the word
of God in that God is at work in our situation calling
the church into the future. The church has indeed
always looked to the future and has derived much
of its energy from the hope of this future. Now it is
being called to move toward this future and actively
share in the process of transformation so necessary
to bring it about. This kind of involvement in a
rapidly changing and developing Africa requires a
new missionary style and approach. For one thing,
the African church will have to be characterized by
foresight, that particular capacity to estimate, with
a sure instinct for the future, the trends that will
affect the church of tomorrow. It will have to antici-
pate the future not out of curiosity, but out of es-
chatological hope, knowing as it does that God
never ceases to draw near to his people, inviting
them to the absolute future. This means that the
church will not only have to scrutinize the signs of
the times and listen more attentively to the winds of
change; it will also have to take universal grace
more seriously into account than in the past. Its
plans, therefore, will no longer simply be drawn up
on the basis of the church's material resources and
human possibilities, like those of any big corpora-
tion. Rather they will be determined above all by
the presence and actual workings of Christ in the
African situation. Wherever Christ is on the move,

the church must plan to be there with him—even if it means considerable readjustment and inconvenience. Only an attentive, listening church is capable of this.

In the past missionaries were above all people of steadfast faith who had their minds firmly made up about everything that really counted. They knew exactly what they had to do and teach, how they were to do and say it, and why they were doing it in the quickest, most direct way possible. The moral solutions they prescribed were clear-cut, the questions they might be asked summarily answered, and the people they served quickly classified. On the whole, listening was not part of their missionary makeup. In fact, busy missioners usually considered listening something of a waste of time; they had more important things to do. Today missionaries must be people of dialogue, and that means above all people who can listen. It is difficult to convince missionaries, dedicated as they are, that they do not really communicate with their people. But the fact is that they often don't really even care or seek to communicate: What they call their wish to communicate is only a face-saving way of describing the wish to "hear themselves speak," to make their listeners more attentive, so that their missionary vocation will seem as valid as ever. Thus, when they claim to have made contact with someone, they are really only saying that the echo chamber has worked, that they have heard coming back to themselves the echoes of their own preaching.

In the future, if there is to be a future for the church in developing countries, missionaries will have to listen fully, and not just select or pick out for reception only what they want to hear or are willing to accept at any moment—those elements that suit them in one way of another, reassure them or at least do not disturb them. To be sure, there is a real risk in listening attentively, with understanding and empathy: Our lives are shaped by those we listen to—and by those to whom we refuse to listen. The more one tries to understand others and their world as they experience it, the greater the risk of being changed oneself. The risk of being changed or deeply influenced by the very people one has come to evangelize is perhaps the most frightening prospect any missionary can face. Yet if universal grace is taken seriously, then clearly missionaries need not be afraid of being changed or influenced by the people they serve. On the contrary, they will welcome this influence, knowing full well that they have not come to these people merely to bring something, but also to receive something for themselves as well, something for their own faith and hope. In this way, missionaries become living signs of hope, which in turn become the hallmark of the missionary church. Only people of hope can really listen. And by listening attentively, they evince that kind of openmindedness that recognizes the true variety of God's gifts in people. If encouraged to develop according to their own best tendencies, these in turn will involve faithfulness to the God of grace. To the extent, therefore, that missionaries see themselves as listeners, as seekers, and learners, they help to animate and bring to fruition God's universal grace. To this extent, also, they work for the future of the church in developing countries.

Existential Approach

There is another, more existential, approach to our initial question. Instead of asking, "Will the church have a future in modern Africa?" we can reformulate our question thus: "Will the church be *present* in the New Africa and, if so, what will this presence be?" Here we must distinguish between two senses of "presence."

Taking an example from our childhood experience, we all remember sitting in a classroom while the teacher made the roll call. When our name was called out, we answered: "Present." We might have been half asleep or distracted, but we still mustered up enough response to register that we were present. The teacher recorded our physical presence and assumed, rightly or wrongly, that our mind was also available to communicate with. Or again, taking our cue from the vocabulary we commonly use, a person suffering from a mental disease is often referred to as one who "is not all there." This is a strange, but telling expression. True sanity is defined as the personal quality of being fully present in any given situation and at any given moment. I am sane when I am all there. When we say that people are present—more present than others —we mean, in the first place, that they are more capable of experiencing things, more enterprising, more able to cope with the world than others are. True presence, however, lies deeper. It is the exquisite ability to be drawn into and involved in the lives and destinies of other people. To be present means to exist-with-others-in-the-world.

Thus, when we ask the question: "Will the church be present in Africa in twenty or fifty years from now?" we are not asking: "Will the churches still be standing? Will the number of Christians have significantly increased? Will Christianity be as visible as it is today?" To be present does not mean simply to be "here" or "there": A stone is here or there, but a stone is not present. Presence is a spiritual phenomenon, implying an active relationship and a great response to people's needs and deep aspirations. If Africa rejected colonialism from its bosom, it is mainly because the colonial powers were not really *present,* that is, their physical presence did not sufficiently correspond to the greatest needs and aspirations of the African people. Whether or not Africa will one day disown Christianity as it did colonialism depends on the church's readiness to pay the required "bride-price" for the privilege of being present and working in Africa. Although the actual cost of being present is difficult to assess, one thing is certain: Before trying to spread the Christian faith, the church itself will have to make a great act of faith in God's universal grace, as well as an explicit act of reparation for having so long failed to recognize the workings of grace on the African continent outside its own visible boundaries. Only on condition that the church is genuinely ready to acknowledge and work with the original grace that is the heritage of the African people can it realistically hope to have a future in Africa. This deep-seated conviction must underlie every Christian commitment, inspire every spoken word, and animate every missionary encounter. In short, it must be more than a mere theological opinion; rather, it must become a working principle rooted in the whole missionary structure of the church, behind which is the divine energy of its mission. If the church is consistent with itself, this conviction is bound to affect its pastoral and missionary approach. We suggest that the following areas of practical concern should be among the first to undergo radical change.

Ecumenism. Division among Christians has always been a scandal to the Africans, who have naturally a strong sense of the unity of life. Nothing has weakened and confused the meaning of the gospel more in Africa than the divisions and rivalries between the Christians themselves. Since their arrival in Africa, the various Christian denominations have been competing with one another, much like Russia and the United States in their race to the moon. Not only did this entail costly duplication in many areas, but the race itself was strongly motivated by pride and the desire for prestige—a frantic effort to prove to the Africans that one denomination was better than the other. This invariably gave rise to what has been aptly termed an "edifice complex." Each denomination built its own schools, its own hospitals, its own printing units, and so on. Mutual support was neither offered nor accepted. It was as though each denomination was bent on going it alone. Each seemed more intent on developing its own little "religious bantustan" than on developing the nation which gave it hospitality; each more concerned with how it would survive than how it could serve.

The concept of universal grace precludes any such ghetto mentality. It not only gives rise to the ecumenical movement but prevents our search for Christian unity from becoming simply a passing fad or a vague, formless idea. The ecumenical spirit must be for all of us an abiding attitude, a permeating atmosphere, a milieu in which we work and think and have our being. It must become for us what water is to a fish—the only medium in which we are truly at home. Outside of it, we should feel most uncomfortable; outside of it, we fear we may die.

Africanization. When and if the idea of universal grace is taken seriously, the prospects of Africanization will be greatly enhanced. This does not merely mean replacing the missionary bishops and clergy with local clergy; it also means developing financial self-reliance and, more importantly, self-reliance in thinking and planning church policy. The Tanzanian bishops, in their centenary message, made the point strongly in Swahili which, when translated, asks: "Is it not a thing of shame for a grown man to go back to his mother to take suck from her still?"

The blame for the slowness of the church to Africanize has been generally placed on the expatriate missionaries, and African priests and ministers are particularly prone to lay the blame squarely on their white colleagues. It must be admitted that in spite of their truly impressive achievements, the expatriate missionaries did little or nothing to develop an African liturgy, music, theology, and pastoral style of approach. Yet, even with the best of intentions and under the best circumstances, could they reasonably have been expected to do so? Is this not an area in which Africans alone can and must make their contribution? Unlike ecclesiastical positions and posts of responsibility, which can be so easily turned over to the Africans (often with a simple stroke of the pen!), Africanization cannot be transferred—much less handed over on a silver platter. If it is to exist, it will have to be created by Africans themselves, and this requires inner freedom and resources of creativity and imagination that cannot be supplied by others. Like any real creation, Africanization will require of the African clergy much more hard work and inspiration than is generally admitted, or else it will be nothing more than a "cheap imitation." The success of the African Independent churches in this area proves beyond any doubt at all that the required spontaneity, independence, and creativity do exist in the religious soul of Africa.

The reason why Africanization has not yet taken place is not so much because the expatriate missionaries have deliberately imposed their particular brand and style of ministry; it is more especially because the African clergy have not been sufficiently creative and independent-minded. In their earnest endeavor to "live up" to standards, they have unconsciously tried to think, talk, live, and conduct their ministry in the same way the white missionaries did. They did not dare to be different because to be different somehow meant to be inferior. Thus in their efforts to prove themselves "equal," they could not really be true to themselves.

In order to overcome this lingering feeling of inferiority and this sense of inadequacy, the African clergy too must be converted to the truth and reality of universal grace. Universal grace does not admit a rigid standardization of the ministry; in fact it not only recognizes the priesthood of all Christian ministers but also allows and encourages a wide variety of different styles in the ministry. Flexibility is essential in the realm of God's grace. Hence, if universal grace is taken seriously, there is no need to copy or imitate someone else's conception of a good priest or minister—only the need to move toward thinking one's own thoughts, creating one's own style of ministry and, in this case, being as truly and deeply African as one can be. Behind this daring self-confidence, which is one of the basic conditions of creativity, lies the conviction that God never repeats himself or does anything twice in exactly the same way. Rather, God is forever creating something new, something different, and above all something special.

Collaboration. Along with ecumenism and Africanization, the price-tag on the church's future presence in Africa will also include the need to work in much closer conjunction with governments, civil agencies, and international organizations. In the past, whenever the church discovered a temporal need, it went ahead on its own and tried to fill that need the best it could. Where there were no provisions for education, it built schools; where medical facilities were lacking, it built and ran clinics; where there was little or no social welfare, the church stepped in. Today, the situation is quite different. The independent states and governments have effectively taken over. These secular powers, whatever their colors or flag, are becoming keenly aware of the welfare of their people and are better able to promote it. The church should not begrudge this move toward secularization. Christian temporal works remain necessary, but they can no longer be autonomous. Clearly, they must be integrated into overall national plans for development. It would be a mistake for the church, or even Christians working together, to draw up their own plans and projects for development independently of those set out by the government authorities. Hence, when the church discovers a real need in the community, its first question should be: "Is this a need that the church should try to meet, or would we serve the community better by bringing it to the attention of a civil agency in the community better equipped than the church is to meet this need?" Thus the mission and obedience of the church effectively takes place in the context of society and the world. To this extent it becomes a servant church and need never worry about its own survival or continuing presence.

Urban Ministry. As we have already indicated, there is an urgent need for the church to specialize and concentrate on growth and focal points—e.g., the African city. If the church is to be present in the New Africa, it will certainly have to be present in the African cities, where the destinies of millions are at stake. By 1982 there will be some fifty million urbanized Africans. Considering this accelerated process of urbanization, the church is faced here with an entirely new world and a whole set of new problems. It must, in the first place, drastically alter its essentially rural pattern of ministry and parish organization. It must also face the moral implications of the break-up of the original tribal structure, the distortion of African custom in the urban context, and such problems as masses seeking a new community in what are often appallingly bad townships, migratory labor, wages that are frightfully below the poverty datum line, overcrowding, promiscuity of every kind, and unemployment. The upheaval and alienation that has resulted from this migration to the cities makes it by far the largest frontier of African mission activity. As yet, however, there are no convincing signs that the church is prepared to meet this challenge or that it is ready for what must surely be reckoned as one of the greatest spiritual encounters of its history. There is little reason to believe that the church will not continue to neglect the urban African for many more years to come.

Theological Approach

In the final analysis, the question of the church's future is fundamentally a theological one. What its future will be depends on what the church really is, and this is basically a theological question. The church can be viewed from without and from within; it has an exterior face and an interior life; it is a society like any other and yet a society like no other. Depending, therefore, on whether one is looking at the church from within (as a believer) or from without (as a sociologist), the answer to the question of its future may well be different. The reason for this difference is important. Unlike Marxism, for example, Christianity is only partially a system of self-reliance: it must also rely on God's continuing assistance. In so doing, it calls upon invisible resources that can neither be predicted nor sociologically taken into account. Thus the external manifestations of the church's vitality are never equal to the fullness of its interior life or the potential of its unlimited renewals. The church may be old, but there is an eternal youth about it that never ceases to baffle those who would predict its doom and disappearance. Hence any valid statement about the church's future must combine the objective observations of the sociologists with the subjective insights of the believers themselves, that is, those who really love the church. There are certain realities in life that one must love and believe in to understand them fully. The mystery of the human person is one such reality; the mystery of the church is another. Only if we love the church of Christ can we speak of it with any real intelligence, or criticize it with any real freedom and hope.

St. Paul, who had both the critical eye of a sociologist and the heart of a true believer, describes the church as a liminal or threshold community. The church does not exist for itself but is the liminal community that witnesses to the truth that all people are "on the way" to full communion with God. Only when it is true to this mission of preaching the good news of Christ's universal grace does it bring a new dimension of power and courage into the world. The grace of Christ is not the private possession of a group or of a religion; nor is it the special possession of the church. It is a grace for all people, a grace open to all people, and especially the poorest, the last. If it is not given to all, then no one can claim it for oneself. The church therefore exists to infect all people with the hope of this grace and to struggle passionately against anything that would jeopardize the ultimate success of God's creation —anything that would stifle the freedom, justice, and peace that the grace of Christ releases in humankind. Christians must realize, as Albert Camus said, that true generosity to the future lies in giving all to the present.